Spirituality

A USER'S GUIDE

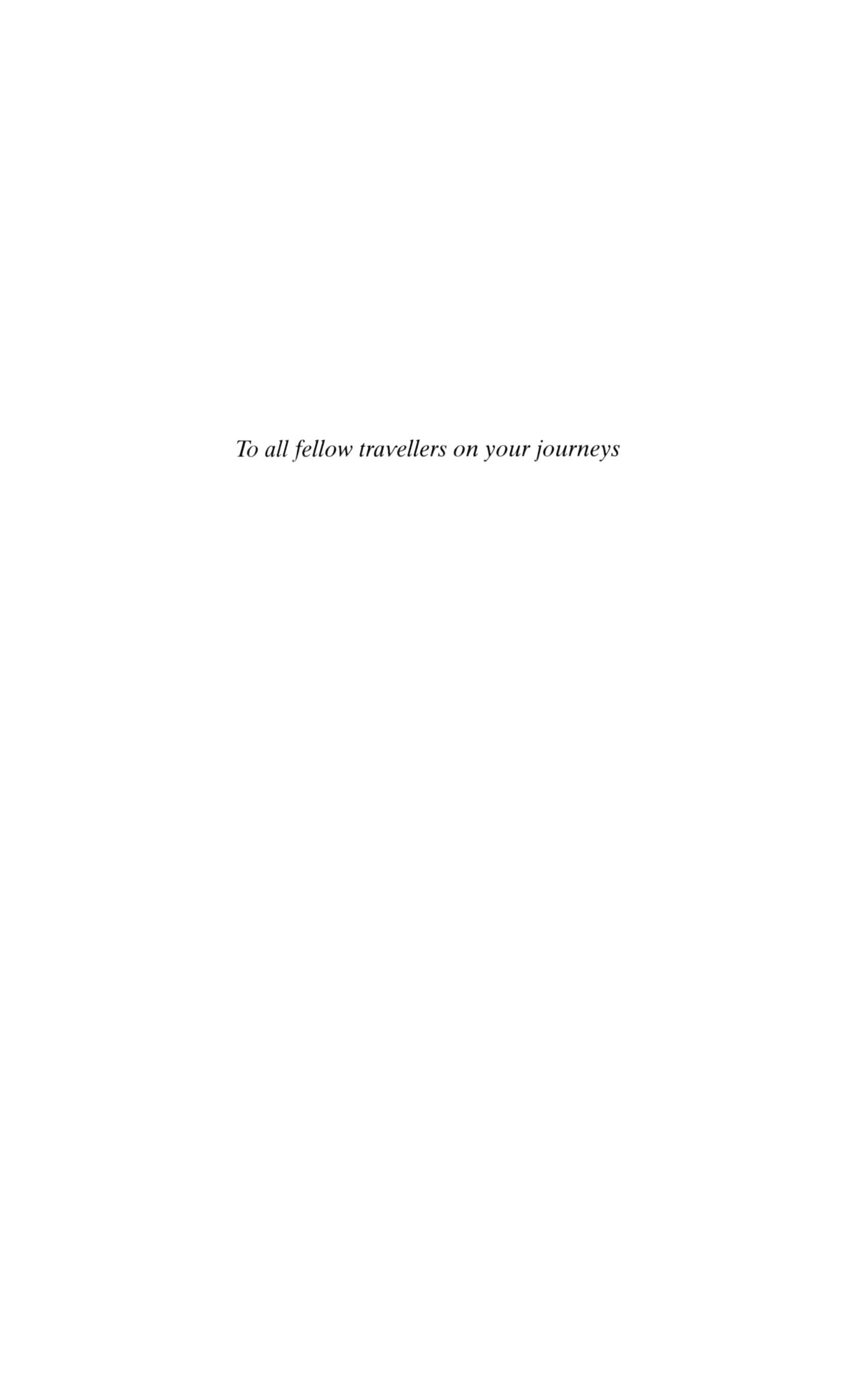

To all fellow travellers on your journeys

THERESE F. HICKS

Spirituality

A USER'S GUIDE

DEEP
STORY
PRESS

First published by Deep Story Press
Wicklow
Ireland

CreateSpace	ISBN: 978-1-911013-91-4
Ebook – mobi format	ISBN: 978-1-911013-89-1
Ebook – ePub format	ISBN: 978-1-911013-90-7
Paperback	ISBN: 978-1-911013-88-4

A CIP catalogue record for this book is
available from the British Library

Produced by Kazoo Independent Publishing Services
222 Beech Park, Lucan, Co. Dublin
www.kazoopublishing.com

Kazoo Independent Publishing Services is not the publisher of this work. All rights and responsibilities pertaining to this work remain with Deep Story Press.

Cover design by Andrew Brown

Printed in the EU

Contents

Acknowledgements

This book has been well over 15 years in the writing. Apart from the wide variety of subjects that I needed to explore in some depth, the pressures of being a psychotherapist, especially for the last eight years of my public employment, have often prevented me from writing. While I did continue to read widely and ponder deeply, the weight of my clients' worlds required the lion's share of my energy. Yet when the context suggested that it was appropriate, my conversations also helped me to frame much of the thought in this work in a way that is relevant to the spiritual wonderings of real people. If they should happen to read what follows, I hope it will provide them with further guidance in their onward journeys.

The earliest origins of this book are to be found in my contact with Rosemary Haughton, initially in her books, especially *The Passionate God*, and later at her women's shelter north of Boston. Her powerful, real-world approach to theology is something missing in the many academic tomes that have provided me with other kinds of information. In the early 2000s, I gave a series of six lectures to an intrepid and adventuresome group of people in Dublin who did their best to take in the mountain of material I put before them. Not being an academic lecturer, I needed some way to articulate the thoughts and reflections that were tumbling around in my brain. With that useful task done, Jeremy Young then volunteered to help me pull together an outline of chapters that would further focus what I was trying to say. From there, I gradually banged out each chapter, needing to finish one before I had any specific idea of where it would go from there.

My conversations with many people have been the refining process that gradually helped me to condense a huge amount of material in a satisfactory way. Some of these interlocutors would be Mairead O'Brien, Nina Dimmitt, Bill Irwin, Mary T. Malone, and Mary Condren. Nina and Jeremy each did a critical read of my first draft, an invaluable gift to any manuscript. An early version of the third chapter was also published in March 2008, in an adapted form, by Luis Gutierrez in his web journal, *Mother Pelican Journal,* devoted to sustainable development.

Chapter 1

A Babel of Spiritualities

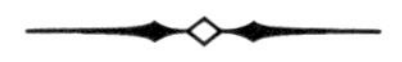

As a psychotherapist I sometimes find myself sitting with a client who has come to the point of asking the most basic question of life: why bother? In their journey through life and their healing process they find that the pain outweighs the promise. In days gone by we had the fear of hell to spur us on (though even that didn't always provide the necessary push). Even more so today, then, for the many people who no longer find the Christian frame of reference and its attendant stories credible, for one reason or another, there comes an inevitable confrontation with the cold, hard question: 'What's it all about?'

It takes a lot of courage to ask this question, and many never do. They are perhaps caught up in pursuits that provide adequate satisfaction or distraction from their inner pain. Or perhaps they make use of the soother of addiction, whether ingesting substances or provoking their own adrenalin to provide that required buzz in life. The current default spirituality is materialism, with consumerism, greed, and constant shopping its main characteristics.

But to be human means to have inner pain. Allowing ourselves to face the terrifying question of whether or not life has a meaning is to stand naked before our pain. But if we do find the courage to ask this most basic question then we can permit life to teach us not only fearlessness but also a deep love for one's self, the basis of a wordless wealth of meaning.

The journey to the awareness of our meaning takes us through many adventures, disasters, and fascinating discoveries. As meaning slowly comes into focus, it gives us the foundation we need to go on living, and the ability to construct a universe that is creative and joyful. This is a daunting task because our own pain can sometimes seem so insurmountable and incurable; in addition, the amount of pain in the world generally is mind-numbing. Yet create a universe of meaning we must, or there is no point in bothering.

However, such a deep and pervasive need for meaning is easily manipulated by those determined to gain power over us. In our eagerness to still this long and lonely ache at the centre of our being, we can easily grab whatever comes to hand, or whomever promises us salvation. In fact, there have been many spiritual paths leading to dead ends, approaches which have been tried and found wanting over the centuries. So I am suggesting that it is very important for each of us to educate ourselves about what is involved in a healthy, psychologically life-giving myth of meaning.

A myth of meaning is another term for a spirituality. It is how we make sense of living and dying. It is what lights our fire and carries us through our darkest moments. It requires both an emotional component – it must grab us – as well as being intellectually plausible. It must not contradict the facts of our known universe. For example, if our known universe contains items of immense age, then a spirituality which tries to tell us that it is only some 6,000-odd years old is simply too contrary to work. But a good spirituality will indeed stretch our rational mind, because the rational mind is incapable of encompassing infinity, and that is what we are dealing with. Thus it is a 'myth' in both senses of the word; it is not a scientifically verifiable recounting of exactly what happened or how things are, yet at the same time, it paints an epic picture that moves us to live fully.

Making a rational choice between spiritualities can be well nigh impossible. Yet making a choice solely on the basis of our emotional reaction to a spiritual path can be very hazardous.

How can we distinguish a healthy spirituality from ones which will disempower us, increase our fear, or give us license to oppress others? Is regarding the planet primarily as a mine of resources for making money a healthy spiritual perspective?

In this book, I am endeavouring to provide guidelines for assessing a functional spirituality. I am not recommending any one spirituality in particular, though I am critical of the dominant systems, especially those which are patriarchal, that is, dominated by men who do not believe that women are equal to them. This is pretty much most of them, either in theory or practice. Perhaps no current spirituality offers us an adequate road map for the twenty-first century. It may still need to be cobbled together from a mix of sources.

In previous centuries, our spirituality was generally determined by our religion; our religion was determined by our family and by when and where we were born. Generations have lived, fought, and died for religions that were not of their own choosing. People have been passionate about the truth of the worldview which they inherited from their ancestors with a blindness of faith that any fundamentalist would envy. But occasionally throughout history human beings have been confronted with the option of choosing their religion or to choose a spirituality rather than a religion. We live in such a time. A religion is a systematized package of beliefs, rituals, and rules which often has a 'them and us' approach. A spirituality is more of a philosophy of spirit, more lightly held, and open to additions and subtractions. Each religion has a spirituality implicit in it, but one may have a spirituality that is not expressed in any sort of religion.

Such times of choice have existed before although often the choice was not exercised in freedom. When the transition from a matrifocal, goddess-imagery-oriented society to a patriarchal, god-dominated society happened, there wasn't really a choice if your only other option was death. But that shift was many millennia ago, and is lost to our general awareness. More recently, around 2,000 years ago, there was a great spiritual ferment, facilitated in part by the exchange engendered through the rise of empires which had spread across continents and cultures.

These gave people the opportunity to be exposed to the religious beliefs of others. Often, there could still be a strong dose of coercion involved in shifting from one religion to another. Nevertheless, some people began to look at the new ideas and approaches, and found themselves drawn to perspectives to which they had not been born. One could suggest many reasons for such a state of affairs. Had the family gods been discredited by military loss? Did the victorious gods impress with their power? Did people want to be seen as being on the winning side? If you were a merchant, was it a surer way to make money? I would suggest that the evolution of human consciousness has contributed to the gradual and repeated outgrowing of religions and their spiritualities.

In the West, from around 200 BCE (Before the Common Era, the same as Before Christ), especially in Alexandria (on the Nile Delta, northern Egypt), centres of learning had arisen to which people of many nationalities came to pursue their curiosity about the questions of living and dying, power and truth. This also included trying to understand how reality functioned, because by this time it was thought to reflect the 'will of the gods'. The more one understood how the gods functioned, the more closely one could know and follow that will. As the various empires – Sumerian, Assyrian, Babylonian, Persian, Greek, and Roman – rose and fell, they had displaced many peoples. Greeks, Jews, Persians, and Egyptians in particular were eager to pursue intellectual and religious traditions which painted bigger pictures than those of their clan ancestors or divinities.

That time of ferment was eventually crushed by the Roman Empire in its death throes in the early fourth century CE (Common Era, same as AD, year of our Lord), when it seized upon a specific form of Christianity to be the imperial religion. The 'Fathers of the Church' ushered in a particularly harsh era asserting their religion was the one, true, and universal religion which all people must follow. This reflected the coming to power of a *thinking*-based consciousness, which specialized in making absolute rules and declaring that it had the universal truth. The only serious challenge to this in the West has been the rise of Islam which has adopted a similarly rigid understanding of its own omniscience. Within both traditions there has been a multiplicity of variations which have evolved over the centuries. Each has been as likely to kill the adherents of its own variants as those of other religions.

It has been this conviction, that one's religion is directly revealed by the one and only god, which has been the basis of such murderous zeal. Many factors would allow a person to operate from such a perspective: a lack of awareness of the history of religions, a lack of awareness of how the human psyche functions, or a deep insecurity which requires certainty about one's ultimate fate. However, as we come to more awareness of both history and ourselves – our need for emotional reassurance, our propensity for projecting our inner processes onto external 'reality', etc. – we can begin to take a more objective look at the phenomena of religion and spirituality.

Using a psychological perspective as the basis for an evaluation of spirituality has received serious support from an unexpected quarter in the past century. The insight of quantum physics has been that no absolutes exist, or if they do, we cannot know them, because of the 'observer effect'. This effect states that all perception unavoidably impacts whatever is being perceived. This means that it is the psyche, and secondarily the organs of sense perception, which ultimately craft anything we perceive. (See Chapter 4 for a more extended discussion.) Our sureness of our own existence has to be taken as an irrefutable assumption. Since there are other conscious beings around us, we must also grant them their existence. But our *perception* of them and ourselves, and our *impression* of who we/they are and how we/they operate, is very much coloured by the condition of our psyche, our level of emotional development, and the intellectual frame of reference within which we navigate.

Thus, the competition to define the psyche and how it operates becomes the crucial question. Many theories abound, starting with Freud and the psychoanalytic school, through all manner of psychodynamic, developmental, systemic, and cognitive behavioural theories, not to mention Buddhist and alternative approaches. All of these are also the basis for psychothcrapies. It would seem that whatever theory produces the best results should be declared the winner. But what you consider to be the 'best results' depends on your ideas about how a healthy human being should look and function. The other difficulty is that all the therapies work for some people, but none of them work for everyone, nor produce the same depth of healing. It is a real Gordian knot of interactive factors.

However, the multitude of psychological theories pales in comparison to the number of religions and spiritualities now available to an educated or well-informed person. There are not only those which have been around for at least several centuries, but in the past 100 years the appearance of what may broadly be termed New Age spiritualities has exacerbated the situation considerably.

Any book which endeavours to propose guidelines for the evaluation of spiritualities is of necessity written from the perspective of the life experience and education of the author. This is another one of those inescapable limitations which could make one frozen with a sense of inadequacy. Hopefully, however, acknowledging this state of affairs will prevent the reader from taking what is presented (or anything else) as gospel. Rather, it is a contribution to a dialogue, which is central to the project of being human. The more experience a person has, and the broader one's perspective, the more one brings to the conversation. The importance of such conversations to the evolution of spirituality is that they are part of a feedback loop, which allows each of us to consider the possibilities being experimented with by other people. My own story is thus the next necessary chapter, before getting into the myriad of considerations already touched upon.

As will become obvious in the unfolding of this book, there is another aspect of human experience that is a vital component of one's spirituality. This is the inner dialogue constantly running through our heads most of the time, but which many of us never examine directly. We are, in fact, constantly talking to ourselves. And generally, the inner voice is saying negative, self-critical things. But sometimes, we experience a vivid thought coming into our awareness which seems to solve a problem we've been wrestling with, or which gives some direction as to our next step in life. We need to pay attention to this inner dialogue and engage with it in a constructive way if we are to be aware of the deeper part of ourselves that connects us with a bigger picture. It is important to realize that it is another part of our self, not a foreign entity, neither ill nor totally good.

At the end of most chapters, I will provide a more personal account that gives some idea of the ongoing inner dialogue that was at the heart of my journey to finding a spirituality that works for me. Here's a start:

Let me tell you about Ceil. I remember vaguely when I first half-noticed her out of the corner of my eye. I'm pretty sure it was some time during my first year in college, but you know how details get fuzzy as time passes. She was a very quiet person, and shy. I'm not even sure how long she'd been in the class before I was aware of her. Some snide sorts said that she was never really there. Any time they tried to look at her, they said she disappeared!

But with a little gentle attention, Ceil slowly revealed herself to be an incredible being. Over the years, I can now see that it has been a very mutual process of growth and inspiration. As I gradually got to know her, she helped me to see the deep humour and amazing beauty that sits under my nose in the here and now. This has enriched my life immeasurably, bringing me to a whole new understanding of what it means to be human. Yet I can also see that she has benefitted from my awareness. Her ability to express herself, and to participate in a range of emotional experiences, has developed as we have communed together. It is like a flower and the sun, though I'm not sure which role each of us plays. Perhaps we have taken turns in a dance of deepening exchange.

Generally, Ceil seems to manage a rather even keel in herself. For the most part, nothing seems to perturb her at any great depth. But there have been times when her inner anguish has become palpable. When that happens, the ache in my chest is so severe that I think my heart will burst under the pressure of such pain. You wouldn't think that one person could contain that level of suffering. Yet on the other hand, she has also revealed moments, even days, of incomprehensible ecstasy. I imagine that is what is meant by enlightenment or samadhi.

It is these experiences of deep interaction with Ceil that have made the most significant contribution to my sense of my self and the meaning of my life. After having been touched by such moments, there is nothing that could ever again make being human anything less than a miracle. I mean, to simply be there, to watch events unfold, to be aghast at unexpected outcomes. All this is happening day to day to day, though not on the type of screen which absorbs most people.

Many people have been aware, at one time or another, of someone like Ceil in their lives. But the number who extend this inner vitality any thought, or who even suspect that there might be something there worth pursuing, is sadly very small. What of you? Have you noticed some dynamic like this in your life?

Chapter 2

Autobiographical Sketch

Spirituality is the story we tell ourselves to make sense of living and dying. Not just rational sense, but also emotional sense, is required to make a credible story. The story that appeals to us very much depends on the story that is our individual life. So let me share my life story with you, so you can understand my particular perspective on spirituality. If it resonates with your own story, you may find this book useful.

I feel fortunate to have been born into that great wave of American humanity known as the 'baby boomers'. With the end of WWII, hundreds of thousands of soldiers returned home to start families, and produced a huge surge of children. My father made the most of the US government's funding of education for these discharged soldiers, known as the GI Bill, and opted for a college education. This was something he would never have been able to otherwise afford, yet to which he was well suited. Eventually he became a full professor. Both my parents were progressive Catholics in their twenties and thirties, critical of a Church that didn't live in their real world.

Baby boomers had an active social agenda as they began to challenge nearly every aspect of society, especially its social and economic oppressions. It was a wind that was blowing throughout a world horrified at the atrocities and devastation of WWII, which had come hot on the heels of WWI. There was a sense that things had to change to prevent further wars. Amazingly, there was a strand of this energy within the Roman Catholic Church. A compromise candidate became Pope John XXIII in 1959. Not expected to live long, he subsequently died in 1963, but not before he surprised everyone and convened a council to bring the Church into the modern world. It became known as the Second Vatican Council, and was seen by many as an opportunity to undo the damage of the First Vatican Council (1870), not to mention the Council of Trent (1545–63), among others.

The vast majority of US Catholics, including my parents, breathed a sigh of relief as English became the language of their Mass, religious education for adults was introduced, ritual practices were updated, and there was an effort to recognize adult Catholics as precisely that – adults. Previously adults had been treated like children under the direction of 'Father', but as the level of education of the general population began to rise, there had been a lot of dissatisfaction with this paternalistic approach.

The Second Vatican Council (1962–65) happened during the latter half of my primary school education. So as I started high school, there was a wave of change in both the Church and in society. It was the 1960s – flower people, guitar masses, Vietnam War protests, and civil rights marches were the order of the day. I was not much involved in the social side of the upheaval, mostly because I had been a peer-group reject, and was busy surviving my own experience of social injustice. Because of this social isolation, I had decided to explore the matter of God to see if there was a reason for living. Otherwise, it was checkout time.

My story is thus profoundly impacted by the timing of my birth. I was born into a generation determined to change the status quo so that the horrors of war and fascism would be banished for all time. The Catholic Church sought to renew itself in the spirit of Jesus and the early Church, with its concern for social justice and the valuing of the ordinary person. Clericalism and hierarchy were being challenged by members of both the laity (some now better educated in Scripture and history than the priests and bishops) and the clergy themselves. Thousands left the priesthood and religious communities. When I went to a Roman Catholic university, I was met by vibrant, enthusiastic, and questioning men and women renewing themselves and their Church with great dedication and courage.

As I look at the Catholic Church now, after the impact of John Paul II and his functional agenda of undoing Vatican II, I consider myself to be extremely fortunate to have met the Church during that time of openness and growth. The integration of a modern awareness with a faith perspective allowed for a powerful blossoming of moral and spiritual development, which challenged the establishment of both Church and society to take the message of Jesus seriously and work for social justice.

As part of my journey, in the second half of my second year of college, I engaged the services of a spiritual director. She was a nun who taught in the theology department, but who also had imbibed the importance of emotional development for the spiritual life. She suggested I go for counselling, to begin that journey to 'know thy self'. Thus I found myself on the doorstep of another nun (whose Irish community I would later enter and leave). That was the most pivotal experience of my life. Each February of my undergraduate years had found me visited by deeper and deeper bouts of depression. By the third year, I was suicidal, and, after escaping my parents' home, was on the verge of becoming psychotic – quite a challenge for a trainee counsellor. But Sr. Conchita rose to the occasion, and I have lived to tell the tale. The approach she used was humanistic, simply focusing on helping me to feel my feelings and tell my story in a self-reflective, non-judgemental way.

With a new sense of meaning and of connectedness to other people, an ability to reflect rationally on emotions, and a systemic understanding of human development, I completed an undergraduate degree in theology with a strong component of philosophy, having started in engineering. Yet even at that stage, I began to realize that my original hope, that philosophy asked the questions and theology answered them, was in vain. In my senior research seminar the professor had set us the question: What difference did Jesus make? I began to wonder what use one person being tortured to death on a cross could be to the rest of us. The insistence that it was to pay back the debt humanity owed God because of Adam's sin certainly did not make sense if God was supposed to be all loving. I spent my time in Toronto on an MA programme in theology trying to work this one out to my satisfaction. My thesis for the degree examined Anselm of Canterbury's exposition of this theologically central conviction.

Of course, academia is not set up for the personal exploration of one's own questions, but rather for learning what all previous theologians have said, and demonstrating that you have done so. This didn't really appeal to me, and I began to focus more on a bit of wisdom I had heard: you get to be like the people you live with. Academia, with its brutal politics and heady distance from emotional health, no longer made sense to me as a career path. However, the vibrant energy of the missionary sisters I had met when they answered the doorbell on my weekly visits for psychotherapy, now spoke to me in a very positive way.

Along with counselling, I had begun the journey of persistence, which is meditation, in my second year of college. Although managing to do it every day and staying focused was no easier for me than for any other beginner, I did start to experience what I described as a sense of presence of a loving God, and a passionate interaction with Jesus. The usual agonies of one's twenties provided more than enough topics for reflection and periods of resigned silence. The missionary community I was drawn to had a spirit of simplicity, a great spirit of adventure, and a deep sense of a loving, non-judgemental God. I recognized that I still had a lot of emotional growing and healing to do, and figured that community life was ideally suited to the task. Never a truer word.

While not universally true, most communities of women religious had grasped the opportunity of Vatican II and were engaged in the challenge of incarnating love within their communities and their ministries. This move was well served by the use of psychotherapy and various other tools, such as the enneagram, a Sufi tool for understanding personalities. These promoted emotional growth and a depth of interaction not previously possible in religious life. This missionary community generally lived in small groups of three to six in Africa, which made community interaction all the more intense. So when I arrived in Nigeria in 1977, I was plunged not only into a level of culture shock that was disorienting, but I also grappled with small group living at the back of beyond.

This had the effect of breaking open my experience of reality to a degree which probably would only otherwise have been possible had I been using drugs. My meditation practice deepened immensely as I struggled to keep my balance in an environment on the one hand rich with new possibilities, yet on the other severely different from all I had previously known. This enforced a profound isolation. After a year and a half, I found myself overwhelmed, and returned to the States. But two and a half years later, having reconstructed myself to a greater depth, and with the African reality having become familiar and cherished, I returned to share with others what was meaningful to me.

In Nigeria, I had been working with secondary school students who were boarding, often at considerable distances from their homes. English had to be used because they all spoke different languages. They also had scant knowledge of their local traditions. In Cameroon, however, I found myself working with adults who were still very much in touch with their ancestors. Luckily, in West Cameroon they spoke their own 'pidgin' English, a language which selects some English vocabulary but uses local syntax to order the words. It is easy to pick up, and is used by everyone in West Cameroon, since their local languages have a limited geographic range.

One of my activities was conducting Scripture groups with adults. I continued my practice of starting with Abraham, because he is the first specific ancestor of Jesus, and so is easily related to by those who honour their own ancestors. Having benefitted from asking questions myself, I encouraged group members to ask as many questions as they liked. After we had made our way through the stories of Genesis and Exodus, we came to Leviticus. It was at this point that one fellow asked the crucial question: Look! Here are all our traditional sacrifices in the Bible! Why aren't we allowed to use them?

Having never needed to ask this question myself, I had no clue how to answer it. I suggested they leave it with me, and I'd get back to them. On we went through the rest of the Hebrew Scriptures, and then into the Christian Testament. There, as I was preparing for the meeting in which we would look at the Letter to the Hebrews, I found the answer: Jesus is the last sacrifice and the last priest. Now there is no more need for sacrifices or priests.

No more need for priests.

Part of the struggle of women religious in those days, was the unsatisfactory situation which required them to import a priest for the community Mass. This wasn't so bad if there was a priest about who was in tune with the community's spirit and focus. But in more remote areas, where options were limited, this could be a problem. So this sudden refocusing of my awareness on priesthood struck a vibrating chord in my consciousness.

On my way back to the States after that year (1982), I was able to consult the recently published work by E. Schillebeeckx (1980) entitled *Ministry*. It is a history of Christian ministry, in which he refers to an opinion of Augustine that Christian elders should not consider themselves priests. Priesthood was either a Jewish or pagan practice, and not seen as compatible with a Christian awareness. Each Christian has been baptized into the priesthood of Christ, and has no need for a mediator to God otherwise. It was only in its power struggle with political leaders of the Middle Ages that bishops declared themselves invested with a spiritual power of priesthood, 'different in kind, not just degree' from a baptized Christian.

Thus the people of Cameroon converted me. I unexpectedly had to look at the reality of what Jesus was about, and what the Church was about, and realized that they were two very different things. But I very much loved living and working in Africa, and the community there had become my family, my biological family having already started their drift to becoming right-wing Christian fundamentalists under the influence of Ronald Reagan and later Fox News. So I decided I would not take this theological detail too seriously, and went on my first assignment to Ghana.

There, I continued my practice of using the local traditions to illustrate the evolution of the Christian understanding of God and history. I also continued to reflect on that question as to what difference Jesus had made. Then one day, it suddenly hit me: I was God as Jesus was God! At the time, what I understood by this was that, in terms of my overall being, I was just as divine as Jesus. There was no difficulty understanding Jesus' divinity because it did not differ from that of each person. Rather, how I now saw the significant difference between Jesus and myself was that his *humanity* was more developed. Jesus had been more fully human than others. This was the difference he made: he showed us what a fully functioning human being would look like. This involved accessing a level of 'power to heal' that most people have not yet come to.

At first I thought I must have made a mistake in my reasoning. But no, there it was, the fruit of my deepening spiritual life and theological ponderings. Again, there wasn't anywhere to go with that, but it did feel as though I had finally answered that seminar question.

In February 1985, however, as I was sitting at the celebration of another sister's fiftieth anniversary of profession, I suddenly knew I couldn't continue in the Church any more. It was as if a switch had been flipped in my being. I found this really unnerving and deeply distressing. Yet there was also a calmness, knowing that this was the right thing to do. Rather than immediately bolting, I remained in Ghana till that September, writing *A Bible Reading Guide for Ghana* as a summary of my work in West Africa. Then, with a heavy but steadfast heart, I returned to the States.

In my last year in Ghana, I had been introduced to the work of Carl Jung. This had given me a bridge between my spiritual experiences and psychology, and I thought I might write theology on the basis of Jung's approach in the same way that others had used the writings of Martin Heidegger, a German existentialist philosopher. So I moved to Boston and went in search of a Jungian analyst to get this new venture under way. My life was in bits. I had no relevant qualifications for work, I only knew one person in the whole city, and I had left everything that was meaningful to me. It was a good time to go into analysis, which is an in-depth form of psychotherapy, using dreams to access unconscious feelings and needs. After the first six months, I woke up one day and realized that I was no longer a Christian. The whole notion of a God-out-there no longer rang true.

Another experience in Ghana, which was to have a profound impact on my life, was a kundalini awakening which occurred on retreat in May 1983. This refers to the rising up of the energy which lies coiled at the base of the spine, contained there by the blockages which build up as we deal with emotional injuries in early childhood. There is an entire branch of yoga dedicated specifically to awakening this energy. I hadn't heard about anything like it at that time, and so when the surge of energy happened, I thought I was losing it. In addition, the retreat director with whom I was working would not have been aware of such a phenomenon either, since it is not part of a Christian frame of reference.

Fortunately, my analyst in Boston had been a Sanskrit scholar, and raised the possibility when I mentioned some difficulty dealing with energy roaring around my body. She gave me a copy of Gopi Krishna's autobiography, *Kundalini: The Evolutionary Energy in Man* (1974), in which I discovered there was a precedent for what I was dealing with. My experience was not as powerful as his, but it was in the same ballpark. From there I began to experiment with the energy, gradually following it more deeply into altered states of consciousness. This was an expansion process that required me to turn to New Age understandings of reality in order to find adequate language for my experience.

Since 1986, I have been experimenting with various New Age approaches, incorporating what has been useful, and discarding that which hasn't. Perhaps one of the most challenging transitions was coming to grips with the notion of multiple lifetimes. Initially when I encountered people using such an idea, I demurred that I had enough to deal with in this lifetime, and didn't feel up to taking on others. But slowly, as I shed the worldview of heaven and hell, I realized I needed some construct, some story, for what happens after I die. I had also experimented with some past life regressions, and found them useful. And perhaps most pertinent is that, since reality is a social affair, and I was associating with those who used that frame of reference, I found it more and more congenial.

In 1992, I had started attending a New Age adult education centre in Boston, and thereby had become part of a group learning how to do energy healing. Here I found people on my wavelength, and practical assistance with my abundance of energy. The instructor had been through the Barbara Brennan School of Healing, which meant that the notion of spirit guides was also part of the picture. This made sense in terms of the conversations I had been having in my head since I had moved out of the Christian sphere.

One of the members of the healing group also trained people in reiki. As I got to know her better, she told me about Perelandra, a nature research centre, with its healing tools, spirit guides, and flower essences. I had already discovered flower essences, and had been using Rescue Remedy to good effect. My guiding principle is: if it works, use it. I don't worry about the theory of why it works, assuming that due consideration has been given to both long-term and short-term effects.

My time in Boston was one of immense growth personally and professionally. During 1990 and 1991, I had done an MA in Counselling Psychology and got a job as a psychotherapist working with people with major mental illness. This allowed me to explore the workings of the psyche at a significant depth, and alerted me to my skill as a therapist. But in late 1994 and early 1995, I began to have very vivid dreams about being with various members of my old community in Dublin. The dream would always end with an energetic group hug, which woke me up.

After having invested a lot of time and money in dream work, I couldn't just ignore these powerful experiences. So I thought perhaps I would investigate some of the New Age communities in Massachusetts. I began to do so, spending first single days visiting, then weekends staying with them, reminiscent of my initial contacts with my previous community. On the way home from one such weekend, however, I had this strong sense that my community was still in Dublin. So I booked a ticket for the end of May 1995.

It had been more than eight years since I had been in Dublin on my journeys to and from Africa, and I found it a rapidly changing place. Building cranes peppered the Dublin skyline, new roads were being built, and the power of the Church was noticeably diminished. I reconnected with my friends in, and some now out of, the community, and found myself energized in a very powerful way. One friend in particular encouraged me to seriously consider moving to Ireland. On my flight home, I made my decision.

The logistics of such a move were daunting, however, since Ireland had had a long history of exporting people rather than taking them in. And the differences in the professional structures of psychotherapy were mystifying and off-putting. In the end, I took a job as a nurse's aide in a psychiatric hospital. Even with that, I was only granted a work permit due to the persistent help of another friend.

In September 1998 I finally moved to Dublin. Once again I experienced massive culture shock, but also a deep sense of having made the right decision. Almost immediately, I began to find more pieces of the puzzle on which I had been working. A friend introduced me to Paddy McMahon's *The Grand Design* (1987–1996). I had read extensively in the New Age genre in Boston, but here was a book which contained all the basic commonalities of alternative cosmologies, in a simple, user-friendly, plausible way. I also attended the energy healer and a psychic my circle of Dublin friends recommended.

The transition was a challenging one, however, so I was fortunate to find another excellent Jungian analyst to assist me in my growth and explorations. I was also accepted into a group training to be Jungian analysts. Pension considerations interfered with my completion of that option, but contacts there in turn led me to the Institute for Feminism and Religion. My interaction with this group finally reunited me with my primary interest, and stimulated me to revisit my long-postponed book-writing impulse. The latest puzzle piece to come my way was Michael Newton's work on 'life between lives' (*Journey of Souls*, 1994). I did a life between lives session, and found that it further intensified my sense of meaning, and of having made the right choices for my self throughout my life.

It is from this place of over 45 years of self-exploration, study, and asking questions of life and others, that I have come to my present point of view. Therefore, given that so many other people today are joining the search for a spirituality different from the one they were born into, I am offering the fruits of my own search in the form of four guidelines for how to assess a healthy spirituality. A spirituality needs to:

1. increase one's sense of being loved and loving 'all that is';
2. decrease one's sense of fear;
3. subscribe to social justice; and
4. hold an ecologically responsible point of view.

In the remaining pages I will share how I came to these four guidelines and what they mean more specifically.

Understanding the history of spirituality is particularly useful when trying to assess any one of them, because often old approaches appear under new guises. There has been many a dead end that has been revisited in later centuries, and many pathological convictions which continue to appeal to people whose level of woundedness and self-awareness are in inverse proportion. If my conclusions or recommendations can be of assistance to you as you wonder which way to turn in your spiritual search, I am pleased to put my experience at your disposal.

Chapter 3

What Does It Mean to Be Human?

> *The stream is clearest near the spring. Whatever use may fairly be made of this image, it does not apply to the history of a philosophy or belief, which on the contrary is more equable, and purer, and stronger, when its bed has become deep, and broad, and full. It necessarily rises out of an existing state of things … [O]ld principles reappear under new forms. It changes with them in order to remain the same. In a higher world it is otherwise, but here below* ***to live is to change, and to be perfect is to have changed often*** *[my emphasis].*
>
> *John Henry Newman, 1845*

This is the heart of the matter: how a person understands who or what they are determines everything else. You may say that how we understand reality is of greater importance. But because of that stumbling block called the observer effect, how we understand what is real is dependent on who is speaking. The starting point for all our speculation on what's out 'there' must be our self-knowledge, or what's in 'here'. Even a chicken/egg approach doesn't work, because **how we picture reality tells us more about ourselves than anything else.**

Given that there are numerous people who wish to contribute to the discussion as to who and what they think and feel themselves to be, our information-gathering process must be a combination of qualitative and quantitative input. Then each of us has the difficult task of choosing the model of being human which most appeals to us as individuals. Many people sidestep this responsibility and let someone else make that choice for them. In fact, the very suggestion that it is up to us to make this particular choice is anathema to most religions or spiritual systems. Instead, they design the playing field and the rules, and then allow us the 'freedom' of choosing. What I am suggesting is that a person should look at the various options, with their strengths and limitations, and choose the one that fits best, or cobble together various bits which work the best for oneself. This keeps us from absolutizing our specific choice.

Choice is the very essence of what it means to be human. Yet if someone else writes the rules and determines the stage, there is very little free choice in it. Take for example the choice presented to Adam and Eve in the Hebrew Scriptures: you can have everything in the garden except awareness, the ability to know the difference between good and evil. What a set up! The maker of their world sets them up in a zoo and says you can do what you like, except be like me. Now of course this is just a story which communicates to Jews (and later, Christians) that their choice is limited to what is on the menu – no challenging the powers that be. This adequately reflected the perceived nature of reality in those days in the West, indeed evidently all days until relatively recently.

On the other hand, due to what Hermeticists (a group which started in Egypt several centuries before the Common Era) would call habit energy, by the time we are adults, we have been inculcated by our family and society to see things in a certain way. Easy examples are racial and gender prejudices, or nationalism. Getting outside this point of view takes significant effort, and a willingness to see things differently. But why would you *want* to see things differently? If you grow up in a homogenous society, the only impetus for disagreeing with the dominant point of view is that, for whatever reason, it doesn't work for you. Generally, for those in power in a society, habit energy works quite well. It is usually those who are oppressed, or who are not accorded equality in all ways, who find it useful to challenge the done thing. (Though sometimes even those in power find a certain emptiness in the centre of their being, which drives them to be dissatisfied with business as usual.) Those in charge usually insist that the reason it doesn't work for others is that those people are dysfunctional – there's something wrong with *them*. It is important to address our dysfunction, which everyone has, without negating the fact that we can question and reject the dominant mindset.

Since the advent of empires in the third millennium BCE, with the rise of the Akkadian dynasty, people have had the opportunity to rub shoulders with others who have a different habit energy. With the empire holding the larger space, and forbidding people from physically fighting with each other within the empire (join the army if you want to fight!), ideas and perspectives have had a chance to circulate in a more neutral atmosphere. This has led to syncretism – the mixing together of different traditions and their stories about the powers that be, or the purpose of being human. (It was not until the twentieth century and the establishment of mass media and advertising, with its ability to control and influence significantly how people think, that this benefit of empire began to diminish.)

Let's look at the various options regarding the human being. Probably the most basic and universal understanding of what constitutes a human being is that we are a combination of body and soul. Apart from scientific fundamentalists, who deny any sort of soul or spirit energy in the human being, and those shaped by their assumption, there appears to be a general agreement on these two parts. The nature of the soul, how it differs from the body, how they work together, etc., are all matters of debate. A very clever phrasing of the two divergent points of view is that we are either a body having a spiritual experience, or we are a spirit having a bodily experience.

Another way of characterizing human beings is that we have four functional levels: physical, emotional, mental, and spiritual. Each of these four aspects is composed of energy moving at a specific frequency band, much as light comes in a spectrum called the rainbow. The physical level moves the most slowly, with gradual increases as one moves up to emotional energy, then mental, and finally spiritual. One could also think of these four aspects as being like the four wheels on a car. We function like a four-wheel drive vehicle (though hopefully without the same level of unsustainable pollution and consumption).

The history of a Western understanding of being human is one that takes thinking as its starting point. How thinking evaluates experience is considered the proper order of priorities. For both the Greeks and the writers of the Hebrew Scriptures, thinking was their primary mode of relating to the world. The Greeks used thinking to critique their gods and goddesses, whereas the Jews used it to absolutize their expression of spirit. Greek thinkers, especially the Athenians, took their identity primarily from being thinkers, because there were many other Greeks who weren't keen on thinking in the same way. The Greek people were numerous, and wielded a lot of power politically. The writers of the Hebrew Scriptures, on the other hand, were part of an oppressed group, and their identity was primarily defined by their group's religion. They needed to articulate their specialness to support their differentness.

Prior to the Indo-European penchant for thinking, people were more experientially and relationally oriented – life was organized around the ritual and sensual experiences of eating, drinking, dancing, birthing, dying, and so on, rather than a thought-out analysis of a situation which had been committed to writing.

The rules of the logic system for the Greeks and the Jews were very different. For the Greeks, Aristotle in the third century BCE had worked out a set of guidelines which we still use today. A thing cannot be itself and its opposite at the same time and in the same way, or if $a = b$ and $b = c$, then a must $= c$, etc. The Greek thinkers did not view their religious beliefs as exempt from the rules of their logic. They were able to criticize their gods for their foibles and excesses. Whereas for the Jews, their thinking was dictated to by the assertions of the stories handed down to them by their ancestors about their god. There were no written thinking-based rules of logic in Jewish tradition. If Moses or Yahweh had said it, then it was logical, and suggestions to the contrary weren't (and aren't) entertained.

The difficulty with both of these thinking approaches is that they become disconnected from the experience of the body. The body becomes something that we think *about*, rather than an intrinsic contributor to our sense of being human. We will encounter the effects of this split later in our discussion.

The Judeo-Christian approach

Let us look at the Judeo-Christian (that is the combined perspectives of the Hebrew Scriptures, otherwise known as the Old Testament, and Christianity) thinking on what it means to be human. I will go further and use the Roman Catholic articulation because it is the one with the most extensive history of exposition, and, in its most recent publication, the most traditional and least influenced by modern thinking. My main source for the Roman Catholic position is the *Catechism of the Catholic Church* (1992).

In brief, it sees the meaning of being human as being in relationship with its god. On the surface, this seems benign enough. However, the god which it goes on to describe is highly problematic. While initially said to be entirely loving, the fine print reveals a god who demands serious retribution for any affront to his honour. This is said to have been taken to the point of killing his own son. (See J. Young's *The Violence of God and the War on Terror*, 2007.)

This picture is based on the stories handed down from an earlier time which were gradually expanded on and reinterpreted using thinking from Persian, Babylonian, and Greek writing. A 'salvation history' is described based on the religious experiences and state history of the Jewish people. They felt that their god, Yahweh, had saved them from slavery in Egypt, and promised that they would be a 'kingdom forever', with a particular dynasty (David's) always on the throne.

Unfortunately for them, the development of empires in the Middle East, and later in the Mediterranean world, completely wiped out their kingdom and dispersed their population. This caused a deep crisis of faith for the Jews, who started to re-interpret their understanding of their god in various ways, especially from 600 to 100 BCE. Nationalist aspirations were one form of this thinking, and several 'freedom fighters' emerged with varying degrees of success. (See the First and Second Books of the Maccabees – only found in the Roman Catholic version of the Hebrew Bible because it was originally written in Greek.)

But others were reflecting deeply on their spiritual tradition, and honing it with insights gathered from other traditions. These were woven together to form a separate Wisdom tradition, not the same as the Wisdom literature in the Hebrew Bible and its Greek translation (the Septuagint), which did not depend on the political aspect of their traditional stories. They were beginning to see that their god was more concerned with the quality of life lived and human interaction, especially social justice, rather than military or political success.

One teacher of such wisdom was Jesus of Nazareth, who caused a stir, and was one of a number of wonder-workers who lived between 50 BCE and 75 CE. But his critique, of both his own religious leaders *and* the Roman Empire's economic exploitation of Palestine, led to his execution. His followers continued to experience his presence, however, and his message began to gain support among Jews and Gentiles alike.

He apparently did not outline a complete explanation of his spirituality or his self-understanding as to his mission on a cosmic scale. We are beginning to see that right from the time of his death his closest followers disagreed about how to explain him. These disagreements have more recently become accessible to us due to both textual criticism of the canonical writings as well as recovery of the variant writings that the winners had tried to eliminate. The 'canonical' writings are called the New Testament, and the variants come mainly from the Nag Hammadi texts, discovered in the mid twentieth century.

There was extensive conflict and violent interaction among the numerous Christian groups in the second century. In the early fourth century, the Roman emperor, Constantine, who could see the political potential of the Christian religion, demanded that the leaders of the various factions gather together and settle on an orthodox position. From that time onwards, there has been a standard of orthodoxy against which other interpretations of Jesus were judged, and their proponents expelled or executed. This allowed for the development of a body of belief that followed a particular line of thought.

One of the primary dynamics within the Judeo-Christian tradition is the practice of having a scapegoat. This is a mechanism which allows the group to deal with an angry, judging god. Ritually, an actual goat had been used in the original tribal society. The sins of the people were put on the goat's head (symbolically), and it was driven out into the desert to die (see Leviticus 16). This saved the people from having to be confronted with their sins. But later, people were used as scapegoats. Late first-and-second century male Christians started to use women as the primary scapegoat, projecting all their discomfort with the body, especially their sexual energy, onto women (see M. T. Malone's *Women and Christianity*, 2000). Sexual energy, as you may have noticed, makes it very difficult to think straight, and so was public enemy number one for the male leaders in the Christian communities.

If you look at the current *Catechism* you will notice that running through it are themes related to redeeming humanity which their god had judged as sinful and deserving of everlasting punishment. The official saviour/scapegoat is Jesus, usually called 'Christ' which means 'the anointed one' (indicating, in the Jewish tradition, the king). But even with his death there is uncertainty as to the safety of individuals from damnation, so there is much discussion as to who is 'saved' and how they can be sure of this. The impact of this is very serious. As J. Young has outlined in his *The Cost of Certainty* (2004), the need for certainty in this understanding of being human generates a lot of fear. For all its talk of being saved this practice of judging and scapegoating has made Christianity a violent and fear-enhancing system.

There have been dissidents within the Christian tradition and there is a long history of schisms large and small. (See S. Moncrieff's *God: A User's Guide*, 2006 for 15 double-columned pages listing all the various Christian churches and sects.) More recently within the Roman Catholic Church there have been movements like liberation theology, small Christian communities, and feminist theology which have tried to return to the theme of social justice which they see Jesus as championing. But this has been firmly rejected by the male leadership until recently. It remains to be seen what inroads Pope Francis I will make on this, but the authors of the catechism have decided to take the formulations of the Middle Ages in the science and philosophy of those times as the only acceptable framework within which to talk about Jesus and the meaning of being human.

However, there has been a lot of development in human knowledge since the Middle Ages. Especially since the seventeenth century, there has been a concerted effort to look directly at the evidence of physical reality and human behaviour. This, of course, still suffers from the limitations of the observer effect, but it has helped us to be more precise and objective about what we *say* we are looking at, and who we are. This contrasts with theology and philosophy which rely either on divinely revealed 'truth', or opinions that have been *thought* up by philosophers and theologians.

One may ask why one point of view is not just as good as any other, no matter what century it comes from, given the difficulty of the observer effect. While it is true that we cannot achieve an absolute statement of facts, we can nevertheless look at the impact on the emotional health engendered by the different ways of making meaning of human existence. Most importantly, in the last half of the twentieth century, psychologists have been able to discover the conditions required for emotional health and balance in human beings. It is called attachment theory. It is a theory in the same way that evolution is a theory. (See later in this chapter for further information on it.)

The challenge of how to deal with fear is that whatever we use must work, as much as possible, equally well for all people at the same time. This means that the practice of scapegoating, which certainly helps the person projecting their fears onto someone else, obviously doesn't work well for the person being projected upon. Or, we can ease our financial difficulties by buying the least expensive item or amount of food. But if it is produced at the expense of the exploitation of someone else's labour, or of the environment in an unsustainable way, then it will not ultimately reduce the amount of fear that we will have to deal with. Attacks on the US because of its economic oppression of other countries, or the impact of global warming on local weather, amply illustrate this.

The psychological approaches

A thinking-dominated approach seriously limits our understanding of being human. Thinking operates from the neck up, and has evolved to generally ignore our bodily and emotional realities. Emotions in particular seem to be foreign territory to the majority of people who rely primarily on thinking (who also happen to be men, 60 per cent according to the research; see p. 44). It has been those trying to care for people with emotional problems who have turned their thinking to working *with* emotions rather than trying to eliminate or ignore them. Initially, this often gave us an intellectualized version of the reality of emotions and emoting (for example, Freudian psychoanalysis). But gradually, there have been theorists who have allowed themselves the adventure of trying to think from *inside* their emotions and body experience. These approaches, which are more grounded in the full human experience, tend to be more effective.

This is why, over the past 60 years, many of the people interested in how to become a happy human being have been pursuing psychology and psychotherapy. As indicated previously, this has been true of myself, and I would like to outline the psychological approaches which I have found most useful. Psychology does not deal directly with the matter of the soul, but some psychologies, principally Jung's understanding of the unconscious, allow for a docking gate with spirituality and soul matters. Developmental psychology, especially attachment theory, is the another area which provides useful insight into what makes us tick as human beings. The body-based treatment of trauma is one further area of psychological research which has made a major contribution in the past 20 years.

The two most important aspects of a psychological system are how it describes health, and how it suggests we might achieve it, which obviously also requires an accurate description of the problems we encounter. In Jung's system, he uses a map of the psyche which includes our body, our consciousness, and the unconscious. Ultimately, health in this instance means a good working relationship between consciousness and the unconscious, which is reflected in the health of the body and mind. While the initial container of consciousness is the ego, eventually a bigger phenomenon, which he called the self or Self, was needed to accommodate the unconscious. The personal unconscious is just that: everything we've forgotten or repressed along the way. But the collective unconscious includes a transpersonal or transcendent reality which connects us with all that is.

At the time of Jung's early writing, there was very little infant observation data available. Freud and others had tried to describe the early stages of growth on the basis of their clients' memories and reports of that time in their lives. But this has proved decidedly unworkable and rife with the projections of Freud and others onto the first five years of life. This phenomenon of projection is another version of the observer effect. It gets in the way when trying to arrive at a useable understanding of what is going on inside the experience of infants and young children. More recent infant observation and longitudinal studies of individuals, by multiple observers who can exercise some check on each other's projections, have proved most useful to date in trying to understand human development.

The amazing understanding that this has brought into focus is called attachment theory (in which I also include attunement). I will briefly describe its findings on how bodies function from birth in terms of their physiologically-based ability to interact with their environment and other people for the rest of our lives. Basically what they have discovered is that all mammal newborn bodies are extremely dependent on their interaction with the mother. The mother, through her body, provides not only nutrition and physical safety, but also programmes the infant body with its basic chemical and neurological regulation via the limbic system. A very young body is not self-regulating, but must learn this from *physical* closeness to the mother. This is why, if separated from the mother and not provided with some adequate substitute, young mammals die, even if given warmth, food, and safety. The more evolved the mammal, the more vulnerable it is. Thus, rats can manage to survive better than primates, though their ability to function and expected life span will be greatly reduced. Humans are most vulnerable of all. Even if merely left alone for too long (how long is too long changes with the child's age), or cared for by a mother who is herself insecure, a child will have a lifelong vulnerability to despair, depression, and anxiety due to the impact of the physical dysregulation which underlies these emotions. If the lack of mothering is more severe, it can lead to self-injury, extreme neediness, reduced ability for intimacy, or even make intimate relationships inaccessible. A very readable book on attachment is Thomas Lewis, et al.'s *A General Theory of Love* (2001).

From this research we can see that mother love and its effective communication to the infant is crucial to an individual's ability to live a healthy life. So rather than being simply a romantic ideal, love is indeed what gives us life. It's not romantic love, or even dutiful attention, but rather the heartfelt attunement to the infant's being that provides the needed physical basis for our ability to relate to ourselves and others. It is the very stark ill effects of a lack of love early in life which makes it possible for us to state that the ability to love, and be loved, is essential to being a healthy human. Any religion or spiritual approach which does not support a love-based understanding of human reality will unavoidably exacerbate the early wounding that most of us experience in life.

Prior to the discovery of the importance of attachment, there had already evolved a stage-based understanding of human development. Briefly, each stage of development describes specific tasks which need to be accomplished by the child with essential help from the environment in order to attain healthy functioning as an adult. The infant needs to feel safe and welcomed into the world. The ability to trust is what is at stake here. The inability to trust is probably the most crippling emotional wound for any human being to try to live with. Later in life this leads to paranoia, very low self-esteem, and great difficulty, if not an inability, to enter into intimate relationships. If the parent has not been *emotionally* forthcoming, no matter how competent in physical and material caring, then the infant assumes they have to take care of the parent emotionally to ensure that their own needs are met. This is the origin of unhealthy caretaking and codependent behaviour in which a person takes care of someone else instead of taking care of themselves. Obviously this requires a balance between self-care and caring for others. But if self-care isn't given at least equal consideration then what looks like love is actually a person's needing to be needed.

Sometime after the first nine months the child begins to toddle. With this newfound physical capability the child starts to explore its world. If encouraged and safeguarded in this endeavour the child learns that they are able to launch out into the unknown and get to know it. If they are inhibited in their curiosity, or find themselves constantly traumatized, then children learn to be timid and afraid of life. Later in life, they have a hard time taking any initiative. This leads to a very passive style of living.

The other hugely important task with which toddlers must wrestle is dealing with their own anger. Anger is a natural response to being afraid or being hurt. Fear happens for many reasons, and is unavoidable for us. It is also a huge surge of energy (as the adrenalin flows), which in and of itself is very scary for the little one. How a parent deals with the child's anger is crucial to what happens next. If the parent allows the child to get angry, throw a tantrum, etc., but ensures that the child is kept safe and not abandoned to this atomic explosion, then the child learns that anger is manageable and not lethal in itself. More often what happens is either that the parent punishes the child for expressing anger, or that the parent's own expression of anger is so explosive that the child learns to be very afraid of its own anger. In either instance, the inability to deal with or express anger generally results in depression. Psychodynamically, depression has long been known to be unexpressed anger turned against one's self. Physiologically, anger is mediated by the sympathetic nervous system. If it cannot be expressed, then the sympathetic nervous system gives way to the parasympathetic nervous system which mediates a collapse response, which is the basis of depression.

After toddlerhood, there are more tasks to be addressed but these first few are the most basic and most important for human functioning. Eric Erikson and Jean Piaget are perhaps the most well known of the early developmental theorists. Their work, however, is primarily based on the experiences of boys and men, so the developmental dynamics of girls and women had been seen to be deficient because they are different from the men in some ways. Interestingly, Carol Gilligan (*In a Different Voice*, 1982) has shown that men are more afraid of emotional intimacy but excel at competition, whereas women are more afraid of emotional isolation, and often see winning at competition as promoting this isolation.

All of these developmental researchers were functioning in a Eurocentric context, which doesn't take into account the developmental dynamics of people and cultures outside of a Western setting. The attachment model, however, has been researched on all continents and with many societies and socio-economic groups. It has been found to be relevant for most human subjects. This makes it possible to generalize about the source of fear in human beings. But how the goals of the various developmental stages are achieved may vary from one society to another.

Western psychology, then, sees humans as passing through various developmental stages which culminate in the ability to love oneself and others. This allows for happiness and contentment, without the use of addictive behaviours, and an ability to deal effectively and competently with life experiences, both joyful and painful. One's level of maturity is assessed by one's emotional and interpersonal point of view, including being tolerant, non-judgemental, respecting of life at every level, and a capacity for empathy and compassion.

New Age approaches

Another point of view on the meaning of being human has gained credence since the 1960s. Many New Age systems take a much larger perspective, seeing our human experience as part of a spiritual journey requiring multiple lifetimes. This is not a totally new point of view, since some form of reincarnation can often be found in traditional religions as well as major religions such as Hinduism. However, its elaboration in the twentieth century has made it more user friendly for Western minds.

The notion of reincarnation does not ensure, in itself, the level of maturity described above by psychology. But when combined with a value system calling for social justice, reincarnation allows for both a lessening of fear about what happens to us when we die as well as a sense of responsibility for living our life as best we can without blaming others for the life lessons we are involved in.

Contemporary approaches to reincarnation, from such authors as Brian Weiss, Michael Newton, Patrick Francis McMahon, and Sylvia Browne, agree on the assertion that the purpose of our many lifetimes is to grow in love, or level of vibrational energy. Love energizes us, while fear turns us cold, sometimes to the point of paralysis. To help us with the hard work of this growth, we are said to have the assistance of spirit guides (perhaps the origin of angels in the Judeo-Christian tradition), with whom we have a long-term relationship. They advise us when choosing the circumstances and goals of an incarnation, but the individual soul (not ego) is thought to have the ultimate choice.

Each lifetime has specific goals, or lessons, for the insights and healing which we hope to achieve. Sometimes we are successful, or perhaps only partially so. Pre-birth our soul sets up circumstances calculated to give us the best chance of achieving our goals. This includes an agreement with those souls who will be our parents, as well as the choice of economic, social, and health details. Lifetime after lifetime, we are confronted with circumstances which give us the opportunity to make spiritually healthy choices. Past life research indicates that we come to these choice points repeatedly until we make the healthy one.

It is fairly clear from the information gained in this sort of research that our personal level of wisdom in the world beyond is not necessarily higher than the one we use here. Despite increased awareness and a much bigger perspective, it is the amount of our fear which can lead us to design unrealistic or counterproductive lifetimes. We can never know for certain, however, exactly what the point of any given lifetime is on this side of the great divide. So no judgement as to the success or failure of a lifetime is possible before it is completed and viewed by the soul involved. If we have learned what we needed to learn while here, then the lifetime was a success, even if it looks wasted or miserable otherwise. The stories, channelled or reported under hypnosis, are fascinating in the creativity used to achieve growth and healing.

The other interesting detail of the multiple incarnation perspective is that we tend to incarnate with the same souls over and over, taking different roles in order to understand life from differing perspectives. Michael Newton's work is very specific in this area, with clients describing a soul mate, a soul group, and soul working groups, who tend to be part of one another's cast of characters from lifetime to lifetime, though not necessarily every time.

This understanding of what it means to be human is at the same time very comforting and very challenging. It eliminates any sense of being under anyone else's power or will. We have set this story up in order to help ourselves grow and heal, and so it is primarily for our good. Yet at the same time, we are challenged to change our emotional and judgemental perspective in order to let go of the fear which confronts us throughout our life. There is no one else to blame for our 'bad luck' or lack of power in life.

The serious 'shadow' side of this perspective is the same as the one which plagues societies which subscribe to reincarnation. It is all too easy for those in power or the wealthy to dismiss the suffering of others as the result of the sufferer's choice for their growth, thus allowing the powerful to continue with injustice and oppression. No matter what scripts people are operating from in their lifetime, it is important for every individual to manifest love and respect for all other conscious beings (and this includes nature consciousnesses). We need to do this, not simply for the sake of others, but for our own sake. It is extremely harmful to ourselves if we do not operate from a level of integrity which understands that *all* our actions and thoughts impact on us. This is why self-love cannot be disengaged from love of others. To paraphrase a reported comment by Jesus, whatever you do to the least of those in society, you do to yourself.

At the same time, this does not mean that we are responsible for other people's self-destructive or unwise choices. If we have the opportunity to help someone to understand how they might be harmful to themselves, it is a good thing to do, so long as they are open to this kind of sharing. But to the extent that their misfortune is due to the systematic oppression of people in a society, we must work to remedy the system. Still, we are not meant to be saviours to one another. Empowering ourselves and one another to know and exercise our creative talents is the meaning of love. Empowerment starts with how we are related to from the time of our birth. Therefore generating and maintaining a society which supports women and men in the job of healthy parenting needs to be the primary purpose of a society, not the increasing of the profits of corporations.

Dualism

Perhaps the most problematic area of understanding regarding being human has been the attitude of spiritual thinking about the body. As I have indicated by various remarks previously, the human ability to think has been greatly developed in the past 4,000 years. This has resulted in significant benefits for us and in some ways has helped us to be less afraid. But rational thinking itself has been afraid of the non-rational aspects of being human. This includes the body, our emotions, and spirit; in other words, all the other aspects of being human. This seems a strange state of affairs, but it is nonetheless amply demonstrated by human history.

With the advent of philosophy and theology in Western traditions, there has arisen the notion that spirit is good and matter/bodies are evil. The religion of Zoroaster, which appeared in Persia long before the Hebrew people started their story, posits a god of light and a god of darkness. Later, it was said that the soul was darkened by its union with the body, or matter. This is the basis of what is called dualism – the notion that there are two basic energies in the universe, one good and the other evil. This would contrast with monism, which states that all the energy in the universe is of the same status and ultimately one. It manifests in different forms, but with no inherent goodness or badness in any of them. The Judeo-Christian tradition has been heavily influenced by dualism, starting from the time when the Jews were exiled in Babylon.

I would suggest that there are several reasons why our thinking perspective is so afraid of life's other aspects. Firstly, thinking allows us to express our self-awareness. It is only thinking that can be self-reflective. Only thinking can know that it is thinking. Only thinking can observe from the outside and say, 'I am having this feeling', or 'I am thinking this thought.' It can also anticipate the future in a way that surpasses what we have personally learned from past mistakes, for example if I pass a car on a bend in the road, I may be hit by an oncoming car.

But then we can also notice that we are alone. The price of being self-aware is to know our aloneness in the universe. (And this is just as true in the spirit world as when we are in a body, based on contemporary research.) There is no one else who can look at the world from exactly the same point of view as myself. Even the most well-nurtured individual must acknowledge that, at the end of the day, they are alone with themselves. The ultimate aloneness that thinking identifies is death. Thinking cannot see beyond this reality which it has constructed, and so death is its greatest fear.

As I will explore at greater length in the next chapter, it is only when thinking manages to allow itself to work with the other aspects of our being can it begin to get beyond its fear. Intuition allows us to experience being one with all that is. When we come to this experience, we can then hold our aloneness in a larger container. It does not eliminate that basic fear, but it does make it manageable.

Mind/body/spirit

The other thing that gets in the rational mind's way is the body. Bodies move at a slower vibration than intellect, as do emotions. The rational mind finds itself inhibited by emotions of fear, derailed by feelings of sexual passion, defocused by boredom or anxiety, and tormented by physical pain. Because thinking has taken a long time to figure out how things actually work, it has traditionally blamed the body and emotions for its difficulties. And again, because most thinkers early on in the human experiment have been men (see Myers, I. B. et al.'s *MBTI Manual: A Guide to the Development and Use of the Myers-Briggs Type Indicator*, 1998), they have scapegoated women as the source of the problem: Women are the route by which souls become bodies; women are the sexual tempters who distract men from the business of war and domination. Men have not taken responsibility for their own bodies and emotions, choosing instead to deny their bodies and project all their sexual feelings onto women.

Contemporary neuroscience demonstrates very clearly how it is that bodies hold emotions. The neural pathways of the body initially are not programmed for any habitual reaction. Repetitive experiences of an emotion cause the body to hold a preference for a particular reaction in a given situation. When we see a drunken parent, we tense up. Even when we intellectually realize that this reaction is no longer helpful to us, it takes us a lot of time and effort to actually change the way our neural circuitry is wired and thus our behaviour. Paul, in his Letter to the Romans (7:19), says: The good I would do, I do not, and the evil I would not, I do! We can all identify with his frustration. Not understanding neurophysiology, men of his time concluded that the body was bad. The body isn't bad; it simply holds energy at a very slow rate of vibration.

But there is an advantage to this. A friend once observed that meeting her pain in her body made it easier to heal. Attending to our bodies, which vibrate at a slower frequency than our emotions or our intellect, provides an opportunity to engage with our pain in a slowed-down state. The slower it vibrates the easier it is to heal. Thinking about our bodies can't heal them. But being *in* our bodies, and connecting consciously with them, allows healing to happen. Recent advances in the treatment of trauma have powerfully illustrated this. (See B. van der Kolk's *The Body Keeps Score* [2014], and P. Ogden's *Trauma and the Body* [2006].)

Thus we come to a spirituality of the body. This provides a meaning for our being here, in a body, with all its limitations. Yet it is not a medical model approach to physiology, which reduces the body to itself, allowing no awareness of the spirit energy or soul, which is its underlying reality and sustainer. This mind/body/spirit connection is something we are only beginning to rediscover since the 1960s. But finding our way to this level of wisdom requires spiritual maps that far surpass those of the previous two millennia in the West.

Materialism

Although I had been making passing references in the early drafts of this book to the impact of materialism and consumerism on society since the 1950s, I had not originally intended to include it as one of the ways of providing meaning for human beings. But as the years have progressed, it is becoming more and more obvious that materialism, and its correlate, consumerism, is one of the most dominant spiritualities on the planet today.

A more traditional understanding of 'spirituality' would not see materialism as a spiritual path. Yet it is the way many people functionally find meaning in their lives today. It is most ferociously championed by the financial elite, who feel that they are special and superior to those who are not super wealthy, say, one of the top 400 hundred wealthiest families in the world. And because they are 'the winners' in so many people's eyes, we are drawn to imitate them, often without being aware of what we are doing. Yet if you don't prioritize money in a significant way, you are unlikely to survive in the modern world. Without money, one quickly becomes homeless as an adult. Even if your parents decide to let you live in their house, most probably they will die before you, and then you won't have the money to keep the house up. In a modern society, everything is accessed with money: food, health care, education, etc. Without it, death is the most likely and soonest outcome. Yet acquiring enough money to live at a tolerable level requires a lot of time and effort, as well as a certain degree of mental health.

As previously laid out, if we define a spirituality as that story which gives meaning to our living and dying, then materialism ticks all the boxes. It defines the meaning of human life as that which is found only in the literal physical matter of existence. The 'spirit' of materialism is that this is all there is – death is the end. Materialists embrace very literally the phrase 'thou art dust, and unto dust thou shalt return'. In this perspective, it is our interaction with matter that is all that counts. While the matter of one's family, at the very least a set of parents, if not partners and children, may be meaningful in a passing kind of way, the most important aspect of matter is money. The more you make, the more you buy, the better you are. Shopping and consumerism are what give satisfaction to a day and a country. It is your patriotic duty to consume so that you sustain jobs and make profits for the shareholders. And when you make enough money, then you can buy governments and countries.

Today, consumerism is the most common form of social interaction and social identity. People shop to feel good and powerful (retail therapy), and need to have more material goods than they can use or afford. This has inevitably affected the way people relate to life, work, each other, and the environment. Having and consuming, no matter how unsustainable, are rarely ever criticized. It also evidently rules out any kind of challenging of the multinationals who fuel the supply of goods and jobs so essential to people's sense of well-being.

As my father's cousin, himself a salesperson, once noted 'everything must be sold'. For him, that was the basic type of interaction between humans. If you had something that someone else wanted or needed, then money needed to change hands. Even though he could be generous at a personal level, selling was the way he saw the world working. Unfortunately, this has become the driving force in how we relate to our environment as well. The earth is for sale, and, as long as shareholders feel they are getting an optimal return on their investments, nothing else matters, even if the earth is destroyed in the process. People are also for sale, in terms of their labour. Again, it doesn't matter if employees of a company have a constantly deteriorating standard of living as long as the quarter's profits make the markets and the shareholders happy.

Ironically, not only is the planet fair game for selling but even spirituality itself has been made a product, marketed and commodified like everything else. In *Selling Spirituality* (2004), J. Carrette and R. King do an excellent job of articulating the rise of the materialist/consumerist spirituality. I will briefly outline some of their main points. Interestingly, they see psychology, as it has grown since the 1950s, as the initial opening for the development of consumerism as a spirituality. They contend that it was the promotion of the highly individualized sense of self which made personal development and individual preferences the determining factor in a person's understanding of what is important in the world. Any consideration of the common good became totally secondary to *self*-development. Spirituality thus became disconnected from the social fabric of society and the environment, whereas previously these had been primary focuses or at least basic assumptions.

The significant disadvantage of this attitude for spiritual seekers is that it makes them easy prey to modern advertising. Products are packaged as promoting a lifestyle or making a statement about one's spiritual values. Of course, this is another area in which psychology has been a corrupting force in the modern world. A four-part documentary series made for the BBC in 2002 called *The Century of the Self* by Adam Curtis outlines how Freud's nephew, Edward Bernays, in the 1920s used the notion of psychological drives to inform advertising, or 'propaganda' as it was initially called. In this way, not only could 'consent [be] manufactured' by those selling stuff, but also it has been used by the US and British governments to gradually mould their population's perception of the rest of the world. This was called 'brainwashing' when practised by the Russians. The control of the media has thus become an essential part of the mechanism of 'persuasion' exercised by those who rule the world.

After the first shift into the privatizing of spirituality a second shift occurred in the 1980s where sculpting oneself into a being who excels at the making of money was itself seen as a spiritual path. One's success or excellence as a human being is reflected in the amount of money one is able to make. This feeds into what is known as neoliberalism. Its perspective on reality is that

> cultural forms [are] themselves … commodities. For the first time in human history, economics has begun to dictate the terms of expression for the rest of the social world. Now, unhinged from the social to an unprecedented degree, the market is able to dictate the cultural and political agenda and take over the processes of socialisation (such as the cultivation and disciplining of individual appetites) that have been traditionally carried out by religious and state institutions. (p. 44, *Selling Spirituality*)

In this system, Capital is god, the absolute determinant of all social value and economic policies. Even nation states must be subservient to corporate profits, and no natural resource can be withheld from those who would exploit it for the benefit of Capital. One other criticism that *Selling Spirituality* presents is that commodifying spirituality makes it quantifiable, measurable, and assessable by number. A number can now be put on the quality of our human life.

The final transition to the displacement of traditional asceticism is found when it is remoulded into a justification for the oppression of workers.

> When employees are encouraged to 'transcend' material discomfort and consider work to be a sacred activity (as in Emmon's five characteristics of the 'spiritually intelligent' person), we are able to see the complicity, whether intentional or not, between these ways of characterizing the individual and a corporate capitalist agenda. Why, one wonders, is dissatisfaction with social injustice

> and a willingness to resist exploitation not seen as a sign of 'spiritual intelligence'? The answer is simple. Such ideas echo a wider cultural ideology of 'excellence' and 'efficiency' that surrounds the classroom, the office and the markct. It reflects the ideological links between psychology and capitalism. (p. 52 *Selling Spirituality*)

While I would agree with much of what Carrette and King have to say in *Selling Spirituality*, I would contend that their familiarity with psychology has a limitation. Like everything else, psychology has its pros and cons. It is true that the emphasis on self-development has made people more vulnerable to being manipulated by advertising. But at the same time unless we attend to healing ourselves, we will be unable to resist advertising effectively. Precisely because our deepest insecurities and fears compromise our ability to make free and healthy choices, it is essential that we find ways of healing these deep wounds. But not every theory or description of human psychology is capable of doing this, so it is important to find ones that do. When we have learned how to love ourselves adequately so that our fear is minimized, and our neediness no longer dominant, then, and only then, will we truly be able to engage in social justice and ecological responsibility. Before that, our fear will trump our ideals.

Summary

To end this chapter, let me review these four approaches to what it means to be human: Judeo-Christian, psychological, New Age, and materialism, also noting some of their pros and cons.

The Judeo-Christian tradition has allowed rational consciousness to emerge and get to know itself by developing a dialogue with its god. Its downside is that it also reflects a fear-based approach to reality which characterizes the ego and rational consciousness.

The psychological understanding of the human has mapped out our stages of growth, helping us to understand how our fear works, and what to do to heal it by also describing models of emotional maturity. It suffers from the limitations of the modern scientific point of view, except for that of quantum physics, which does not deal with any reality apart from the physical. This leaves out any consideration of the spirit level.

The New Age point of view introduces a wider cosmology, which places the project of being human in a bigger picture which is more congenial to many contemporary minds. It deals with the questions of fear and evil in a more empowering way. Its drawback is that it tends to be easily manipulated for selfish ends. Social justice is not well developed in its various presentations.

Materialism has helped us to live more comfortably, with a longer life span and better health (if you have the money). But its overall disadvantages so far outweigh these advantages that it is difficult to truly give much credit to this approach. After about 5,000 years of keeping records of debt and demanding repayment, we have come to the brink of destroying our environment to the point where the continued existence of humankind is in grave doubt. Accountants have kept records so that money can be made from the earth, but have not kept track of the cost of generating mountains of toxic waste and oceans of pesticides.

There have been a number of pivotal points in my life. Each has built on the previous one, so I suppose it would be best to start with the first one I recognize. It was in my third year of college. At the beginning of that year, I had started meeting with a psychotherapist. She was actually still in training, which meant she took a lot of care with our interactions, knowing her limitations in ways that somewhat more experienced therapists can forget.

I had been referred to her by a woman who was helping me to explore what was then called the 'spiritual life'. Starting in the 1960s, and aided by the Second Vatican Council, many people had become aware of the intimate relationship between emotional health and spiritual health. This had taken the focus off sin and suffering, and shifted it over to the more positively oriented journey of learning how to love oneself and others. I had taken a moral theology course in my second year, which looked at the parallel between emotional and neurological development, and a person's understanding of right and wrong. On this basis Lawrence Kohlberg, a psychologist, has worked out what he describes as 'stages of moral development'. This outlines that how a person understands morality changes as they mature psychologically.

Emotions, however, were very foreign territory for me at that time. I had grown up in a family, as the eldest child and only daughter, with a very emotionally repressed father, and an emotionally intrusive mother. This is a very difficult environment in which to grow into an emotionally balanced person. In addition, my innate way of relating to reality is through my intellect. This is great for getting ahead in school. But in terms of being able to relate to other people, it has a lot of drawbacks. The way I found to cope with the emotional imbalances of my parents was to adopt my father's way of going – simply repress the emotions!

So when I started meeting with the psychotherapist, she often found herself saying, 'Yes, I hear that is what you think about this, but I asked you how you feel about this.' It took me six months to even admit I had emotions. This was tricky stuff. At some level I knew I was sitting on top of a pile of pain, and human defence mechanisms are well designed to keep us from meeting up with it. Gradually, however, I slowly engaged with some of how I was feeling.

Then one day, after about nine months of conversations with the psychotherapist, I was with two other people on campus, having a conversation about something or other. In the course of our exchange, I slowly recognized that there was a subtext of emotion in the conversation. This was the first time I had ever registered such a thing. I was astounded. I could now see that how others felt about a topic significantly shaped their opinion on the matter. It was like having lived in a black and white world and suddenly registering colour.

That was a really important turning point in my life. It allowed me to connect with other people at an emotional level, and to understand their experiences and thinking in a whole new way. Without having turned that corner, my life would have taken a very different course, probably a much darker one. The ability to connect with one's self and others emotionally is a basic component of emotional health.

Chapter 4

Letting Go of the Need for Absolutes

Rational thinking has many uses, and is important for helping us to deal with our emotions productively when they get out of balance. But it can also become the tool of our insecurities, and used to construct realities that primarily respond to our often-unconscious fears. In a world of arbitrariness, it is also handy to be able to say to someone, 'This is the truth!', win the argument, and feel very sure of one's self. This is perhaps easier to see in hindsight, especially in areas like science. For years scientists rejected the possibility of continental drift, and laughed at people like Alfred Wegener and Arthur Holmes who championed it in the first half of the twentieth century. Now it is commonly accepted.

Truth wasn't so much of an issue when a goddess was the accepted form of divinity. The realities celebrated then were very self-evident: women were pregnant, babies were born, and people loved, laughed, suffered, agonized, and died. Shamans communicated with the invisible world, found game for the hunters, and healed the sick. They discerned the name of a child, as given by the ancestors in the spirit world, from which the child had just come. People recycled on earth much as the plants and animals did. No explicit doctrines or beliefs were necessary. The force of life was the only one exercised. No one fought over who was right or wrong, over whose child an infant was, or over the control of land. The number of children was regulated by women not to exceed what nature could provide to hunter-gatherers. The community pooled resources so there was enough for everyone.

A child belonged to the mother who had borne it, and to the ancestors who journeyed with the community as much as anyone else.

But since the activity of abstract thinking began to gain popularity and power in the eastern Mediterranean during the first millennium BCE, there has been the difficulty of determining who is right in their thinking about the nature of the deity, or the deity's will, or how to relate to the world of spirit. These things were no longer self-evident. Still, those who are convinced that they 'know the truth' often have a hypnotic effect and power over others. Thinking begets questions, which reflect uncertainty – not knowing. Uncertainty attracts fear – what if I am wrong, what if I am rejected by my god, what if I lose out and die, what if ...?

Bad luck or ill health or untimely death now must have a cause, a reason that gives us the power to avoid it. And in fact, much has been gained in length of life and ease of living as we have struggled to understand and take control of our world. But as we are constantly reminded, the need to be right, the need to be sure of the truth as determined by 'God', has led to the bloodiest and most brutal of human activities. Once we begin to believe that there is an absolute truth, revealed by *our* god, then we are simultaneously the happiest and the most miserable of beings. The happiest because we are saved from our fear by the power of our god, and the most miserable because we can never be totally sure we have satisfied our god, generating another fear.

Perhaps the reason for this is that our god is actually a projection of our own being. This is blasphemous to a true believer, but is becoming more and more obvious to the rest of us. So who is right? Many gods and goddesses have come and gone, with no ill effect on the world in their passing. So do they exist? Does anything exist? What is really real?

It has been commonly accepted in the West that the reality we bump up against physically is the really real. Anyone who discounts that is considered to be out of touch with reality. So the scientists, sensing victory, got down to analysing this really real stuff. Gradually, they managed to build microscopes that went deeper and deeper into molecules, then atoms, and finally subatomic particles. And when they got to the bottom of it all, they discovered that ... there was nothing there! But wait! Where did solidity go?

In the past 100 years there has been a scientific revolution every bit as staggering as the Copernican Revolution. Copernicus said that the earth was not the centre of the universe. This was greeted with outrage and ridicule at that time: 'Is it not obvious that the sun moves around the earth?' In the twentieth century, there has been the quantum physics revolution, which has largely been ignored, except by quantum physicists. Even biologists and chemists still operate as if it hasn't happened. Very simply put, the quantum physics revolution says that what we perceive has been crafted by our minds, or psyches. This is known as the 'observer effect'. If confronted by this assertion, the 'ordinary' person would be quick to dismiss such a perspective. The film *What the Bleep Do We Know?* has been the most accessible communication of this revolution to date. It does a good job of explaining how quantum physics understands the observer effect, and how it works.

Basically, as the scientists got to the smallest pieces of reality, they discovered that the very act of trying to perceive something actually has an impact on it. The act of 'looking' at something changes it. The first instance of this is called Heisenberg's uncertainty principle. Werner Heisenberg discovered that we can know the position of a particle *or* its velocity, but not both *at the same time.* The next major blow was finding that an electron can be either a wave or a particle, depending on how it is looked at (see T. Hartmann's *The Last Hours of Ancient Sunlight*, 2004). Before then, waves and particles had been considered mutually exclusive expressions of energy.

At a physical level we need light to look at and see something. But light itself is a bundle of energy. When it bounces on something which is of a similar size to itself, it affects and changes the thing we are trying to see. At an emotional level, we project internal organizing patterns and emotional energy onto other things (and people). And at an intellectual level, we also depend on traditional ways of organizing our incoming perceptions which are based on previous experiences (autopilot or habit energy).

So the observer is just as much a part of the event being looked at as the thing itself. What makes energy seem solid is the force field around it. When we bump into something, we are encountering its force field. What we see or feel or sense otherwise is that part of its energy vibration which our five senses are narrowly focused to detect. But even after that our brain and then our mind have to *interpret* what is arriving as electrical impulses into the biological brain. The field of Gestalt psychology studies how the mind organizes what is perceived by its senses.

There are a number of good books which are more or less successful at helping the ordinary person come to grips with this discovery, that what we experience as reality is actually the product of our psyche. Deepak Chopra's *SynchroDestiny* (2003), Arnold Mindell's *The Quantum Mind* (2000) and *Dreaming While Awake* (2001) are three I recommend. Another is Fred Alan Wolf's *Mind into Matter: A New Alchemy of Science and Spirit* (2001), and I am borrowing the following example from his work. It is part of a much more extensive discussion but is useful for experiencing the observer effect.

The Necker cube

Louis Albert Necker (1786–1861)

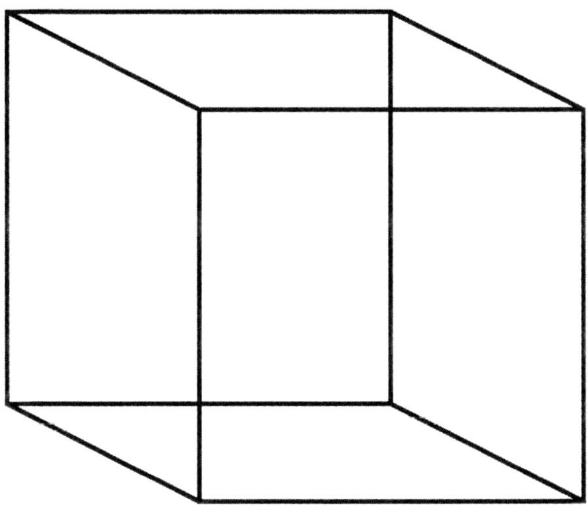

If I ask you to look at the above illustration and identify it, most of you would say it was a cube. But if I ask you if you are looking down at the cube or up at it, there would then be a difference of opinion. I could affirm both points of view, but could also ask for yet another option. Eventually, someone might say, 'Triangles, rectangles, and quadrangles', recognizing that they are just flat pieces bordering each other on a flat page.

Such an optical illusion is an excellent illustration of the observer effect. How you look at the thing affects the reality. You can't see the 'looking up' and the 'looking down' at the cube, nor even the flatness, at exactly the same time. When the thing shifts, is it shifting on the paper, or shifting in your mind? Which view is the true one?

This type of illustration, that is, an optical 'illusion', is generally value neutral. Emotionally, it doesn't usually make a difference to you how you look at it. You have no vested interest in whether it's below or above you. Unless, of course, you can only see one of the options. Then you could get quite upset at the assertion that there's more than one way to look at the thing, if you fear being wrong, inadequate, or different. But there are topics which provoke a lot of intense emotional reaction, and the view of the deity is one of them.

The need to be absolutely sure about God and his will is the haunting problem of Christianity. Jeremy Young has written a thorough reflection on this in his *The Cost of Certainty* (2004). Basically, he looks at how the conditional love of God for humans is set out in the Christian Testament with its assertion of a 'day of judgement'. Both on the day we die, and at the 'end of time', those who have not believed in Jesus as their saviour *and* repented of their sins will be sent to everlasting hell. This is a very serious threat if you buy into the overall system.

The only way most people can adequately cope with this view of reality is to project their fear of not being good enough onto other people. Others are ignorant or lazy or dirty. Behold the scapegoat dynamic again! Everyone else has to believe in this view of reality as well or they may undermine the security acquired by those who are convinced that they 'know the everlasting truth'. In addition, those who claim to control the forgiveness of sins acquire huge market control. Thus we also find in the Christian Testament a passage, generally agreed to be a later addition to the text, in which Jesus is shown to be giving just such power to his follower Peter who won the struggle to rule the early Christian communities (Matthew 16:18).

What I am suggesting, however, is that the **fear and insecurity** which drive people to find 'the truth' are **an offshoot of the evolution of consciousness**. The development of rational thinking, along with all its immense advantages, also leaves us at the mercy of its inability to deal with the bigger picture: infinity. Reason cannot grasp the mystical sense of union with all that is which undergirds a holistic understanding of reality. Only intuition can do that.

But in order for the intellect to carve out its space in the human reality, it has had to contend with the fear-based experiences which its own nascent consciousness has simultaneously evoked and identified. It is a circular situation similar to a dog chasing its tail. The dog catches sight of its tail but doesn't understand that the tail is part of itself. It races around in dizzying circles. One day it finally catches its tail and sinks in its teeth. Immediately there is the painful realization that the tail is part of itself. Or perhaps not. Perhaps there is only the puzzled awareness that someone invisible has attacked and caused pain – the devil at work!

This is what rational consciousness is now coming to see. The fear which it has seen as residing in other 'evil' people is actually sourced in itself. It is now possible for the rational mind to understand an additional level of reality. The long night of fear, occasioned by self-consciousness, has finally been given an electric light. We can now see, through increased self-awareness, that it is our very ability to self-reflect which induces our fear. We know our own separation from all that is and it scares the hell out of us. On the other hand, only when we are separate can we know our own uniqueness and specialness.

For those who are able to let go of rationality as the only valid mode of thinking, there is also the ability of intuition which clues us into an awareness that we are one with all that is. This is the only sustainable and healthy solution to the side effect of intense fear inherent in rational consciousness. It is a matter of teamwork. An intuition-dominant mode of thinking can attribute causalities which are not accurate and therefore are ineffective in dealing with practical challenges. An intellect-dominant mode of thinking is unable to understand its own fear and therefore it is projected onto others. These others, or 'not me's', are then attacked or scapegoated. But when the two are used together, each acknowledging and validating the perspective of the other, then fear can be reduced more effectively and an embracing of oneness and love is possible.

In quantum physics rationality has finally discovered that 'reality' is an illusion in many respects. As I said before, it's not that there's nothing out there, but our *perception* of it/them, and ourselves, is primarily influenced by who we are in ourselves. Some perspectives have intuited this insight long ago. In Hinduism and Hermeticism, the view that reality is an illusion, 'maya' or 'habit mind', has long been taught. But without the security of an intuitive understanding of our oneness with all that is, this view is unacceptable to the rational mind. It's just too scary to be accepted. Besides, it must be there, or it wouldn't hurt when we walk into it.

Once we have both modes of experiencing, thinking and intuition, at our disposal, however, we can begin to identify and withdraw our projections. Awareness that the source of fear is consciousness itself doesn't make the fear go away. We will still feel fear and encounter it in a myriad of places. But it has lost its ultimate power and we know we have nothing to fear except fear itself. There's nothing out there that is going to judge us, no problem that can't be solved by cooperation, and no dispute that can't be healed once each party can look dispassionately at the fear which underlies their anger. Once we learn to trust that the universe is on our side, we can accept that even death is possibly only a transition to another state of being.

But this level of understanding and trust can't be accessed simply by hearing or reading about the mechanism of projection, and learning that we sculpt our experience of reality. Only as each person is willing to experiment with this understanding of how reality functions will they be able to shift their fear from an external threat to an inner problem. Projection is also one of what psychologists call 'defence mechanisms'. Most people are unwilling or unable to let go of this tool without someone else's help. Fear is a very powerful energy, not to be underestimated in its ability to 'prove' that it is real. The most effective procedure for dissolving its grip on our consciousness is psychotherapy, which specifically addresses such defence mechanisms without reducing the unconscious to sex, envy or chaos.

One very important spinoff from all the wars perpetrated in the twentieth century has been a whole new understanding of trauma and how it functions in the human body. We have now learned that once the body becomes traumatized, that is, has felt under lethal attack, it will continue to feel under threat until the body has physically completed an action of successful defence against the attack. No matter how much one emotes or thinks or talks about what initially happened, the sense of danger will not be released from the body until there is a physical resolution. Some well-known trauma treatment theorists and practitioners are Peter Levine who developed somatic experiencing (*In an Unspoken Voice*, 2010; *Healing Trauma*, 2008), and Pat Ogden who developed sensorimotor psychotherapy.

The Theological Solution

The need for a perceived absolute to deal with fear has been translated theologically into the notion of revelation. Someone's 'message', intuition, or pronouncement, preferably the older the better, is transformed into divine revelation that enshrines a particular perspective on reality into the absolute truth. This was an idea that came with the rise of the rational mind. It is because this idea responded to a deeply felt need that it has gained so much credence. But as consciousness has continued to evolve, its untenability has become transparent.

The reaction of people who have not yet expanded their experience to an awareness of the dynamics of fear is to retrench to what is known as a fundamentalist position. They staunchly repeat their mantra: This is true because God said so. Religious fundamentalists cannot allow themselves to check their sources. If they try to trace the written 'word of God', they will soon find that it is extremely problematic. The oldest copies of either the Hebrew or Christian (Greek) Scriptures were created either centuries or decades after the events reported. Jesus didn't speak Greek, so already a translation is involved, even if some of the original accounts were from eyewitnesses. (See N. Douglas-Klotz's *The Hidden Gospel*, 2001 for an interesting exploration of an Aramaic gospel.) Recourse is then made to the Holy Spirit, who guarantees the accuracy of the message, reducing the reasoning to a circular argument. Further, with the tools of textual criticism it becomes quite obvious that many hands have had a part in the writing of the Bible and Scriptures, with different points of view and political agendas.

A very clear illustration of this limitation of the Judeo-Christian Scriptures can be found in the First Book of Samuel. The transition from being a group of loosely related tribes to having a king who ruled over all was a very difficult one for the Hebrew people. They had always distinguished themselves from other groups by saying that Yahweh was their king rather than any human individual. They looked directly to the spirit world for their socio-political organization. This is viable for smaller groups but has been unworkable for more complex social entities. Instead, there had evolved in more established countries the practice of selecting divinised individuals called kings who sat on a throne.

As the Hebrews themselves increased in number and became a settled people, they had to deal with this same shift of gears. In 1 Samuel 8 and 10:17–27, the tribes of Jacob and Israel have decided that they wanted a king so they could be like other nations. Through the prophet Samuel, Yahweh declared that this was an insult to himself. By asking for a human king the Israelites were rejecting Yahweh as their king. Yahweh allowed them to have their king but warned them that they would suffer much because of this king.

In the verses running from 1 Samuel 9:15 to 10:16, however, the text states that a human king is Yahweh's idea. He has seen the suffering of his people under attack and given them a king to help them fight their enemies. The compiler of 1 Samuel makes no effort to determine which of these perspectives is the truth. From a more rationally developed point of view as in the Greek rules of logic, such statements are contradictory and only one can be true. Christian Scripture commentators are quite adept at reconciling such lapses of rationality but it seems fairly obvious that they reflect a difference of political and religious opinion within the Hebrew population.

Lack of careful attention to such difficulties within the Bible, which are not uncommon, allows fundamentalists to absolutize a historically relative interpretation of reality. The tools of divinely sourced fear and scapegoating allow them to deal with their personal fear in the way that we have seen throughout history. People hang on to the absolute of revelation because it fills a very pressing emotional need for certainty. It takes an immense amount of courage to experiment with a different view. Indeed, it cannot be done until a particular level of emotional growth has been reached. There is nothing so powerful as fear. But since this mindset is also killing the planet, we can no longer afford to indulge it with political or economic power.

A new difficulty is that sometimes people exploring alternative or New Age spiritualities continue to assume that they are 'really getting to the truth'. The emotional need for surety is addictive and we have been fed on it from both science and religion for centuries. But once you realize that it is all 'just a story' (see Simon Critchley's notion of 'fiction' in *Faith of the Faithless*, 2012) then you are thrown back on your own sense of your self for support. If you haven't got a serviceable enough sense of your self, then you can't let go of the old story. The experience of it feeling truer simply indicates that it works better for you.

Yet how can anyone make do with 'just a story' when they are trying to come to grips with the intense pain and oppression life throws their way? Well, you'd be surprised at how powerful a good story can be even when you know it's not literally true. What it does do is express something that you know intuitively is true. Besides, as the quantum physicists have demonstrated, there can be nothing more on offer than stories. The enchantment of stories, however, can inspire us just as much as the cold hard facts, if not more so! It is self-development that allows us to bet our lives on what we know in the depths of our being. Then we have not absolutes but working hypotheses which we use until they prove no longer serviceable in reducing our fear and increasing love.

Still, because the unconscious forces at work in the human psyche can never be entirely plumbed, we must use some rational guidelines for assessing the story which moves us emotionally. I am suggesting that how such a story deals with power and fear should require social justice and ecological responsibility. (See Chapters 9 and 10.)

My college years were a high octane mix of curiosity-driven intellectual exploration, emotional development, and painful struggles with self-doubt, depression, and periodic collapses that came from trying to do too much. As I read back on my reflections of those years, I am struck by the intensity of my sense of God and my determination to find a way to love others and myself. The traditional spiritual pathways of Catholicism, heavily focused on sin and salvation through suffering, simply did not make any kind of sense to me. But the newly emerging approaches based on contemporary theology and psychology had not yet been written. I was wandering in the wilderness of an uncharted territory. My conversations with God and Jesus sounded much more like the exuberance of the yet to emerge charismatic movement. All things were possible; life was painful and exciting at the same time.

Falling in love with my first boyfriend gave me an important experience of the power of love in its early stages. Initially we shared the same perspectives on life, and many of the same emotional wounds. But as I began to gain another point of view through psychotherapy, our paths slowly started to diverge. I was now actively engaging with my inner pain, trying to come to grips with it, and seeing how it impacted every aspect of my life. As is often the case when someone enters into this level of awareness, I could also see other people's pain impacting on their own lives. Inner pain had become a necessary part of any conversation to be had with anyone to whom I was related. The source of this pain is the lack of adequate connectedness with one's mother in the first months of life.

Attach or die. That's the challenge every infant faces at the moment of birth. That attachment must take place at two levels – physical and emotional. If it doesn't, the infant may literally die physically, or may die emotionally. Emotional death involves hanging on with a false self that only knows how to please other people, but is unable to take in emotional nurturance for oneself. It leads to a conversation like this:

Daughter: Mother, you seem to have a lot of pain inside you. You've mentioned over the years about how difficult it was growing up for you.

Mother: Oh, I remember how lonely I was as a child. I used to long for my father to play with us, or take us somewhere. But he was always too busy. He had a job, but gambled away his pay cheque most of the time.

Daughter: That does sound very painful.

Mother: Oh, but that's all in the past now. I'm very happy with your father.

Daughter: I remember the times you used to talk about how mean your mother was to you, how she favoured your sister Margaret, and always gave her the best clothes.

Mother: Oh, yes, there was one beautiful red coat a neighbour had passed on to my mother. I begged my mother for it but she gave it to Margaret. She said Margaret was prettier, so it would look better on her. I was heartbroken.

Daughter: That sounds really painful.

Mother: Oh, but it's all in the past now. I never think about it and don't feel it anymore.

Daughter: Then there was that time your grandmother gave you a ruby ring.

Mother: Yes, I loved that ring. She gave it specially to me because I was her favourite. I felt so glamorous with it on. I was only 13, but it made me feel really grown up. My mother took it away from me and said my grandmother shouldn't have given it to me. I never saw that ring again. She never

> told me what she did with it.
>
> ***Daughter:*** Oh, so painful. How did you cope?
>
> ***Mother:*** That's all in the past now. It doesn't matter anymore. I've had a very happy, fulfilling life taking care of your father and you children. The past doesn't matter.

My mother had a reputation for being very harsh verbally to other people. She would throw out thoughtless comments that were very hurtful to those around her. This conversation happened when I was 21 and she was 48. I was trying to get her to understand how pain works in a person's life, but this conversation showed me that there was no way she would ever be able to understand. Not long before she disappeared into dementia, a side effect of her Parkinson's, she apologized for how she had treated me. I accepted her apology, but said she had done the best she could at the time.

Chapter 5

Changing Our Picture of Divinity

Our greatest fear is not that we are inadequate but that we are powerful beyond measure. It is our light, not our darkness, that frightens us ... There's nothing enlightened about shrinking so that other people won't feel insecure around you.

Marianne Williamson, 1992

Traditionally, Westerners' picture of their god has been that of a male entity, an all-powerful creator, an all-knowing and infallible judge, with no beginning and no end. It has often been simply summed up as an 'old white man with a white beard, sitting on a throne in heaven'. While generally only Christian fundamentalists would now acknowledge that this is their image of the divine, functionally this is what underlies most believers' thinking. The details of such a divine image actually come from the time in the history of the Jews when they had returned from exile in Babylon. This was the time of new 'revelation' or 'apocalyptic' in the Jewish community because their old picture of Yahweh no longer worked. Their experience of seeing the Babylonian king on a high throne was then incorporated into their picture of their mighty god, Yahweh (see I. Grünwald's

Apocalyptic and Merkavah Mysticism, 1980).

Recently there has been a lot of interest in the 'new cosmology' which is based on how science reconstructs the probable unfolding of the universe from the Big Bang to the evolution of life on earth. It is awe-inspiring as it looks at the details of how elements were formed and at the delicate balance of conditions necessary to produce life as we know it. It is a good example of a story that works: it both accepts the facts of the physical world as we have come to understand them and grabs us with the sheer beauty and intricacy of the dance of elements. Some also see it as a confirmation of the opinion that there must be a creator lest how else could such a magnificent universe happen?

However, there has been a push from certain circles (Richard Dawkins and Christopher Hitchens among others) to argue against any use of a perspective which posits a divine in our cosmology. They are scientific fundamentalists who belittle and mock anyone who is not enlightened by the holy laws of science. While I would agree that our notion of the divine is healthier when it is not seen as being the creator of the universe, I think it is not healthy to eliminate the divine in a spirituality. This is because it leaves no room for something bigger than human consciousness or for non-rational knowing.

It would also suggest that the scientific story is true in an absolute sense. Scientific fundamentalists say that anything which science cannot prove or which scientists do not consider possible cannot be so. This is very similar to saying that only what is in the Bible can be true or that only something sanctioned by a certain belief system can happen. This places a huge limitation on reality, a limitation which is not workable. The default religion of scientific fundamentalism is materialism, consumerism, and hedonism, driven by an unhealed narcissism. Interestingly, these scientists have not taken on board the quantum physics revolution.

What Dawkins and his friends are trying to do is to eliminate irrational behaviour based on religion. What it would lead to is irrational behaviour based on science. Irrationality is an inescapable aspect of being human. It is better to acknowledge this and work with it, than to try to deny it and leave it in the unconscious where it will continue to control us with great subtlety. Western society's fear of the non-rational has in itself led to some of the greatest atrocities on the planet, particularly the oppression of women and the destruction of the environment. Once again, fear has been projected outwards.

As seen in the observer effect, projection is not something we can eliminate. It is better to use the notion of the divine to allow us to talk about what it is we are projecting. In addition, projection is done not only with our fear but also with our power and sense of self. It is interesting that, as the ego began to take shape in a more focused way in human history, there was a shift of preference for the image of the divine as one rather than many. A high god served by its king in a collective society shifted to monotheism, which demanded ethical accountability from the individual. This has gradually led to the rejection of kingship (See R. Bellah's *Religion in Human Evolution*, 2011).

Projection is, in fact, the way we discover ourselves. That which is about to emerge into our consciousness of our self first appears at a collective level in our image of the divine. Again, this is not to say that the divine does not exist. But that the shape of the divine comes from within us, not from a divine 'out there'.

The image of the deity as female at the dawn of human consciousness in *Homo sapiens* is fairly obvious from an examination of the archaeological artefacts. The deity was commonly seen as a powerful woman, not only the mother of the earth, but also the source of all wisdom in the form of arts, crafts, and agriculture. She functioned with little reference to personal concerns of individual humans but safeguarded the tribe's continued existence. In addition to her, there were the spirit energies of the natural world, found in the land, rivers, mountains, and the sea.

It was only with the appearance of the Indo-European pastoralists that a male image of divinity, a sky father god, broke upon the scene. This shift to a male deity seems to have anticipated the development of *rational* (as distinct from *intuitive*) consciousness. Hand in hand with an emphasis on the masculine was the emergence of warfare, hierarchy, and sacrifice as a form of worship of the deity. (See the work of Marija Gimbutas and René Girard.) The high level of fear which rational consciousness makes inevitable has led to the appearance of mechanisms to manage this fear, for example the scapegoat dynamic, or the elimination of non-rational realities, especially life after death and spirit. But as a result we have been swept up in a wave of violence and destruction which far outstrips anything that the goddess was ever seen to have inflicted on human beings. As outlined above, it is only very recently that rational consciousness is beginning to find other ways to deal with its fear.

Religion, more than any other phenomenon of culture, has reflected men taking power over women. Millennia of patriarchal oppression of women have made it an extremely political topic, and religion has often been used to justify that oppression. Any challenge to a male-dominated cosmology is thus met with the fiercest opposition for sociological reasons. I would suggest that the fear of women taking power in society and over their own bodies is precisely why there has been such a virulent resurgence of patriarchal fundamentalism since the 1980s.

As the notion of a goddess figure has re-emerged in the West in the second half of the twentieth century, many men (and women emotionally dependent on men or thinking dominant themselves) have reacted as if the end of the world were at hand. Thus, this particular topic, within a set of spiritual guidelines, is likely to be the most objectionable and the most difficult for many to countenance.

While acknowledging this, I would suggest that the shift away from a male deity will continue to happen because the evolution of consciousness requires it. Two shifts are necessary in our cosmology as we deepen in our spiritual awareness. One is that there needs to be a balance of masculine and feminine energies within our understanding of divinity. Again, this reflects the gradual development of such a balance within a fully functioning human being.

The other is that we need to abandon any sense of an individualized, localized, focused, controlling deity. I would go so far as to say that it is important that we stop using the word 'god' or any focused/focusing term for the divine. This may help us to be more aware of our tendency to project our power and fear onto a superior being which is totally outside of us. Otherwise we cannot move beyond the historically conditioned image of god which no longer serves us well. It perpetuates the violence of the Judeo-Christian and Islamic traditions and social hierarchy. Phrases such as 'the divine', 'the universe' or 'all that is' may be more workable substitutes.

This last requirement is an extremely difficult task to accomplish as the fate of iconoclast (that is, those that forbid the use of pictures for the divinity) movements testify. Both Islam and Judaism have injunctions against having an image of the deity. This is circumvented by the deity being referred to by masculine pronouns in their sacred books, by having only men as a focus of the deity's power and revelation, and the officiant in rituals. Roman Catholicism has raised up Mary, the mother of Jesus, to a very high status, the Mother of God even. She is seen by many to satisfy the human need for the feminine within divinity. Protestantism has firmly rejected even this much watered down image of the feminine within their theology (yet many of them now allow women priests and ministers). The need to project our individuality onto a deity, to make a god or goddess in our image and likeness, is a long-standing and cherished way of relating to the divine as deity.

However, more contemporary senses of the divine are moving in the direction of relinquishing a human or focused notion of the divine. New Age proponents will speak of 'all that is', or 'the force', or the 'life force'. This is only possible to the extent that someone has a felt sense of the transcendent, non-rational, amorphous energy at the centre of their own being. Until people can accept their own participation in the divine, we will be unable to take responsibility for our life and our world.

In recent years, there has been a great interest in mindfulness meditation, a technique borrowed from Vipassana Buddhism. This skill is one of the many benefits the West gained in the 1960s and 1970s from Asian traditions. When a basic practice of mindfulness is developed, it becomes possible to experience this divine energy. It is a balance of masculine and feminine energies, rational and intuitive, universally compassionate, and non-judging. It is also non-controlling, non-directive and yet promotes everyone's highest good.

The Buddhist understanding of no-deity has been a forerunner of a more diffuse experience of divinity but the use of a male teacher as the pinnacle of enlightenment has also led to sexist dynamics in Buddhist communities. Nevertheless, the practice of mindfulness meditation, highly valued in Buddhism, has given them a lead in discerning how the human psyche contributes to one's picture of, and relationship with, infinity.

Perhaps looking at how the image of the divine or deity changed in the past would be useful. In the Greek literary tradition there is the recounting of how the goddess was officially overthrown. They rationalized the demotion of female deities and the ascent of male deities by claiming that the system of kinship bonds and duties, based on the mother, made the establishment of an urban state unworkable. This is enshrined in the Orestes trilogy, especially the version of *The Eumenides* by Aeschylus.

The first step in the transition is taken by Apollo, who claims that motherhood is not the true source of life. Aeschylus has Apollo declare:

Here is the truth I tell you – see how right I am.
The woman you call the mother of the child
Is not the parent, just a nurse to the seed ...
The man is the source of life – the one who mounts ...
I give you proof that all I say is true.
The father can father forth without a mother.
Here she [Athena] stands, our living witness. Look –
Childsprung full-blown from [the head of] Olympian Zeus,
Never bred in the darkness of the womb
But such a stock no goddess could conceive.

(Trans. R. Fagles, 1975, Bantam, line 665 ff.)

This god/man's idea of a woman then goes on to address the Furies, the goddesses in charge of revenge within the matrifocal realm. Athena instructs them:

Here in our homeland never cast the stones
that whet our bloodlust. Never waste our youth,
inflaming them with the burning wine of strife.
Never pluck the heart of the battle cock
and plant it in our people – intestine war
seething against themselves. Let our wars
rage on abroad, with all their force, to satisfy
our powerful lust for fame. But as for the bird
that fights at home – my curse on civil war.
(Lines 867–975)

She identifies the tribal law of talon, 'an eye for an eye', with the

Furies and forbids it in Athenian society. Let all warfare be projected outwards!

Of course, any familiarity with family-based patriarchal systems, for example the mafia, demonstrates that kinship revenge is not inherently unique to relatedness based on one's mother. But claiming that a goddess-based cosmology was incompatible with the rule of rational, civil law was a handy way for men to simultaneously wrest power away from women and take it for themselves. The men saw themselves as the champions of rationality and fairness.

Within the Hebrew Scriptures, only the most educated of eyes (see R. Patai's *The Hebrew Goddess*, 1990) can now detect any trace of the transition from a goddess-based culture to that of the mighty male Yahweh. Their parallel to Athena's birth is found in the creation myth in which Eve is born from Adam's side. Further, what is lost in translation from the original Hebrew is the fact that the 'false gods', which the prophets are continually railing against, are actually the ancient goddess Asherah. And it is only more recently that scholars have uncovered the fact that for centuries BCE, Yahweh, in the lived practice of Judaism, had a wife. The goddess did not die overnight and the current patriarchal system will not disappear any quicker.

It would be useful to look at how our image of the divine has changed even during the period of it being expressed as a male. The Hebrew tradition has helped in the taming of the divine. The raw, unpredictable energy of its god was gradually reined in by the use of treaties, or covenants. Abraham is described as being a personal favourite of Yahweh's. This is not uncommon between a deity and its tribe but it was then incorporated into the notion of the universal god. The downside of this was that the Jews claimed they were the special favourites of the divine, at the expense of other ethnic groups. On the upside, this personalizing of a relationship with the deity gradually contributed to the individual person being valued and seen as unique and not just one of the herd (see Jeremiah 31:29–30).

Next, the Moses story teaches that our behaviour could influence the deity. His god's behaviour was responsive to human behaviour; bad things happened because someone had been disobedient, had broken the laws as outlined by the deity. This put the divine under the influence of the human which created a sense of power in humans, but also placed a huge burden on the human actors to perform correctly. Later, some of the prophets began to indicate that Yahweh actually preferred the poor and oppressed. Social justice began to figure in the concerns expressed by the deity.

Still, it took the contemporaries of Jesus by surprise when he addressed his god on very personal terms. Elements within the Greco-Roman religions would have experienced the deity as a patron, but this would not have had the same level of intimacy which Jesus' use of the Aramaic *Abba* (Daddy), conveys.

Over the last 2,000 years in the West this more personalized approach to the divine has led to a love affair between the mystics and the divine (see St John of the Cross, St Teresa of Avila, Julian of Norwich). The passion of this interaction has been at times eloquent, at times speechless, and at times abject. It has fuelled a perspective which has universalized our natural affection for those closest to us. It has also restored some sense of the feminine and emotional relatedness as part of the divine.

The ineffability of the divine has also been experienced by mystics of all traditions. Even without the figure of Jesus, Sufism in Islam and the Upanishads in Hinduism have taken this route. In Buddhism, mindfulness or insight meditation has been the starting point for this journey. Such developments would seem to suggest that it is the evolution of human consciousness which is the driving force rather than the religion in and of itself. But it has been difficult for most people to relate to an abstract sense of the divine. Generally, people have needed an image of their deity in order to make it relevant and keep it in their mind's eye.

Characterizing the psychodynamics, that is the emotional currents, of the transitions in the image of the deity as being the tension between masculine and feminine energy is fraught with difficulty. This is due to both the common practice of identifying men with the masculine and women with the feminine, as well as the intense disagreements as to how to understand men and women. In practice, however, many people do not make this distinction. This leads to an inability to allow each gender to integrate both energies.

In terms of the basic emotional dynamics of men and women I am opting to follow a psychobiological point of view. This says that in the drive to perpetuate one's genetic material, males evolved skills needed to 'score' briefly with females. This required brute strength, competition, and cunning. Since they were not the ones to carry the offspring and bring them to maturity, this was all that was required of them to succeed in their basic goal.

Females, on the other hand, had the task of protecting and feeding the young to ensure their survival to adulthood. This required them to develop skills – such as cooperation, communication, and sociability – for enduring relationships, since a group is necessary for them to achieve their goal. Whatever the overall validity of this particular theory it does seem to account for the propensity of men to develop their thinking abilities and women to be more in touch with their feelings and intuition.

Given this configuration of male and female psychological strengths, masculine energy has been characterized as goal-oriented, outwardly focused, pioneering, rational, and self-conscious, with domination and aggression being its downside. And feminine energy has been characterized as creative, relational, nurturing, cooperative, and intuitive, with a lack of concern for those outside the family and stagnation being the drawbacks of this energy. Perhaps at some very early point in human history men may have manifested primarily masculine energy and women feminine energy, but in today's world both men and women are capable of, and need to integrate, a balance of masculine and feminine energies.

The interweaving of psychological, sociological, and spiritual dynamics in the image of the divine makes it very difficult to separate out these various strands. However you characterize the differences between men and women, and whether or not you use the terms masculine and feminine, some way to talk about the evolution of the power dynamics between men and women, and its reflection in dominant spiritualities, must be managed.

As I have said previously, our image of the divine serves a number of purposes. It anticipates the shape of our next stage of development by making the deity in that image and likeness. The shift from polytheism to monotheism reflected the development of individuality. The shift from female to male went with the rise of rational thinking. Within the resulting patriarchal frame of reference it has also helped to contain and manage the intense fear which haunts rational consciousness. Violence became divinely sanctioned, but at the end of the day, this solution to fear has been unsatisfactory and ineffective, perpetuating rather than relieving fear. Instead, as self-awareness made use of rational thinking to explore itself, it discovered that a deity defined by love worked better at decreasing fear.

Yet until we realize that as long as we assume there is someone or something out there in charge of our lives or the bigger picture, the less able we are to assume responsibility for ourselves and the state of our world. On the other hand, if we do not have some sense of an energy called divine, then there is no solution to our fear except the various addictions, the most dreadful currently being the addiction to money, seen in the rampant greed which now drives the world economy.

At this point, it is important to remember that the dominant image of the divine is not something that changes in a hurry in any direction. And yet, in order to craft a healthier spirituality, it is important to look at the dysfunction inherent in a male-dominant hierarchical view of deity.

Psychologically mature spirituality

The emotional deepening of our relationship with the divine by Jesus and the mystics works very well for a psychologically articulated spirituality. The developing human ego has been like a very young child, which has had no sense of its own power, or ability to know its own boundaries. A parent-imaged deity, whether that be Mother or Father, has provided that sense of holding and containment essential to defending our organism from the overwhelming fear inherent in an experience of vulnerability and powerlessness. This is the normal predicament for someone with a not yet formed sense of self. In order for a child to develop in a healthy way, however, it is crucial for them to identify with their parents in their strengths, and eventually to understand that they are equal to the parents. This is considered maturity.

While this is known to be an everyday phenomenon at the human level, when applying it to what has happened in the evolution of our sense of the divine, it will most likely provoke very strong reactions among some Westerners. It has always been denounced as the height of hubris for anyone to consider him or herself equal to the deity. Indeed, for a child to try to function as an adult before they have developed certain skills and abilities is the occasion for short-term mishaps and long-term poor mental health. Yet, although a child needs to see their parents as all powerful and infinitely wise in their younger years, they also need to gradually outgrow such a view as they get older. Just as a child matures and outgrows their picture of their parent, so too is humanity outgrowing the image of the divine which has served Western minds until recently.

Scholars who study the intertestamental period, that is the time between the Hebrew Scriptures and the Greek Christian Testament (400 BCE to 100 CE), have noticed that this is very much what was happening within Jewish circles in Palestine. With the influx of other ways of thinking about the divine and philosophy, many Jews could no longer accept the traditions of their ancestors. So essentially, communities sprang up which experimented with new versions of Yahweh. These were considered new revelations, or apocalypses, which could only be acceptable to orthodoxy if they stayed within certain guidelines (see the work of Ithamar Grünwald). Christianity initially seemed to be another such variation. But its later claim to have superseded the Jews as the 'chosen people' led to a parting of the ways with their Jewish cousins.

It is interesting to note that many of the women mystics of the Middle Ages had already begun to intuit the reality of their being divine. One such would be Marguerite Porete, a French woman who, in the 1290s, wrote *A Mirror of Simple Souls*. In it, she spoke of how a soul could become one with the divine. She was burned at the stake for this.

Those who strenuously object to the possibility of outgrowing an image of the divine would seem to be speaking from one of two points of view. Either they have not yet matured to the point where they are capable of withdrawing their projections and owning their power and their fear, or they do not understand that such ownership is the natural outcome of our evolution. Changing our image of the divine is one of the most challenging processes through which we can pass, emotionally as well as spiritually. It necessitates both realizing that the image currently held is not divinely revealed and that there is a difference between one's image of the divine and the divine itself. (See the Death of God movement in the 1960s.)

Letting go of a belief that one's religion is divinely inspired in all its details, or even most of them, happens as we become more aware of how the psyche functions cognitively and emotionally, and as we begin to notice that other religions also make the same claim in good faith. We need to realize that reality has functioned in history in the same way as it does now, that is, no more (or less) magically, or divinely, blessed than our current time.

For we have come to the place anticipated in Genesis: See, the humans have become like God, knowing what is good and what is bad (3:22). In coming to greater consciousness, we have arrived at what people of an earlier age equated with divinity. Yet we are obviously not out of the woods with regard to fear or social justice. So we need to find an image of the divine which works for our times. This involves a level of maturity that makes us responsible for our own spirituality.

With my move to Toronto I was working really hard to keep up with the increased demands characteristic of graduate school. I also had a whole new world of humans to explore and with whom to negotiate. We were three women sharing an apartment, two of us Americans freshly out of undergrad and a Canadian in a PhD programme. Both of them were medievalists, which was a good complement, as theology was done through history. It was from them that I got a feel for the lived experience of medieval Europe, with its constant local warfare, belief systems, and precarious existence no matter what level of society you were in. But there were also the professors in my programme who were often working at the cutting edge of their own specialities. I started to privilege Scripture, seeing it as the source material for what Christianity was all about. The fellow doing Scripture with those of us in the first year of the MA was just back from Rome, where he had worked with the leading scholar of the recently discovered Ugaritic, an ancient Middle Eastern language.

The study of this was shedding new light on the meaning of texts in the Hebrew Bible. We started going for walks around Toronto as part of an ongoing conversation exploring the implications of such new work for my understanding of Scripture and what it was really saying. The peripatetic approach had been rediscovered. We developed a very deep relationship, which one of my apartment mates reflected on in a letter to me in June 1975, as I was finishing up in Toronto:

> I don't know what to say about you and Bill. I know that he was deeply attached to you. Treasure his love, and treasure the love that you can give to him. I don't believe I've ever known a man outside my brother and father who loved me as well or as profoundly as Bill loves you ... I've never found any man who was so willing to share in the myriad of ways Bill has with you. Pure lust has always gotten in the way ... There's a difference between expressing love physically and also just plain wanting a person because you love him and lust. I've known too many men who equate lust with everything. It's not just satisfying their own drives either. They simply don't look deeply enough to see that passion and lust are not quite synonymous. Anyway what I'm trying to say is that it's almost too hard for me to understand you and Bill. I can relate your love to some people I know including my parents who possess a real love for each other, but yet it's not quite the same. Their love is married love for one difference. And secondly, I myself have not totally been engulfed in such a love as yours. I'm happy for you. It's a painful thing to know you must soon separate. But your love has permeated your souls and anything that God has touched need never stagnate ...

A few months later, just before I entered the Missionary Sisters of the Holy Rosary house in Villanova, PA, I wrote the following:

> [I]f I were to die tomorrow, my life would have been worth living. The gift that Bill and I have been to one another, given by God, is more than either of us ever hoped for. And we have hoped for quite a bit. Before I had only hoped and believed

> that it was possible to love someone intensely but chastely. And now I know that it is indeed possible and beautiful and a gift from God. Thank you!

This friendship helped to anchor me in the years that were to come, helping me to know what love is about, and that I am loveable and can love someone else.

Also while I was in Toronto, I encountered Buddhism. I was impressed by the depth of its meditation practice and wondered if I should look in that direction. But on inner reflection, it felt to me that it was missing a relational experience. This was a really important aspect of what my spiritual life was about. With no God figure it simply felt too empty to feel satisfactory to me, at that time. So I continued on, exploring the Christian tradition intellectually and spiritually. The deep passion of my being was not something I was aware of, but looking back, its intensity is striking.

Chapter 6

Creating Our Own Reality

The title of this chapter captures the most complex spiritual task now facing humanity. The suggestion that we create our own reality has actually been around for a long time. The Hindu notion of maya, which says that all reality is an illusion, hints at the possibility that what we encounter in the everyday world is not as rock solid as it would seem. What is known in the West as the 'esoteric tradition' has said the same thing.

The esoteric tradition probably needs some introduction, this despite the fact that it is, perhaps even more than the Judeo-Christian tradition, responsible for the intellectual shape of the modern world. 'Esoteric' means hidden or secret. It has been traced to Egyptian and Asian roots, and first emerged into the Western philosophical discourse in Alexandria in the first and second centuries BCE under the heading of Hermeticism. However, it was only taught to initiates and so was hidden or kept secret from the general population. A very accessible look at how Hermeticism was integrated into Western society over the centuries can be found in Baigent and Leigh's *The Elixir and the Stone* (1997).

Hermeticism takes its name from Hermes Trismegistus, or Thrice Greatest Hermes. Hermes is the Greek god of communication, magic, and leader of souls into the underworld (psychopomp). He is Mercury in the Roman pantheon, Thoth in the Egyptian. He is said to have written a number of books, which are collectively known as the *Corpus Hermeticum* or The Works of Hermes. These books deal with magic, astrology, and alchemy. They present three principles, which are the basis of Hermeticists' understanding of reality.

The first of these principles is that everything is interrelated. 'As above, so below' is one of their mottos. It means that what exists above, in the non-material world, is reflected in what we see around us. It also means that what is happening inside of us is what determines what we encounter in our life's journey. 'As within, so without.' It is the basis of a holistic worldview. The inability to see this interconnectedness is known as 'habit mind' (or 'habit energy') because it accepts the illusion of separateness as real.

Their second principle states that all knowledge must be gained from personal experience. The word they used in Greek for this type of knowledge is 'gnosis'. Gnosis was given a bad name by early Christian leaders. They condemned anyone who disagreed with them as guilty of a heresy which they called Gnosticism. But this principle is also the basis of modern science which requires experimentation to determine what is real as opposed to looking to divine revelation to define reality. Or to put it another way, we need to ground our intuition in the lived, physical world.

Their third principle is that all knowledge must work, that is, it must empower a person to achieve something practical. For Hermeticists, that practical thing was to see beyond the illusion of everyday reality and to achieve union with the universal Mind, 'nous' (pronounced 'noose'). This then allowed a person to change the shape of everyday reality. At this point, the wise person or magus (plural magi, see Matthew 2:1) could work all manner of miracles, great and small. It was based on the realization by the individual of being one with all that is, which evokes or bestows a sense of compassion for all beings.

Much of what is found in Hermeticism is also found in Mahayana Buddhism and early Taoism, especially in its system of magic (see A. Versluis' *The Philosophy of Magic*, 1998). If you look closely, you will see that many of their tenets are also functionally held by quantum physics, particularly the parts about reality being a reflection of the psyche and the interconnectedness of all that is. So it would seem that this notion, that reality is created by people themselves, has been on the mat a long time. We are only just beginning the task of coming to grips with it. You might say it's an idea whose time has come.

The wisdom of keeping this understanding out of the common discourse is that it delays the knife-edge balancing act required to live with this perspective. There are several beliefs which can result from it. One is that people can blame themselves, or be blamed by others, for all that befalls them. For while we do generate the script of our life, the level at which this happens is in the unconscious or the soul. It is only in the last 150 years or so that we have learned that the unconscious exists and how to access our personal unconscious. This level is not under the control of the ego and so a person cannot be held responsible or blamed for what is transpiring. However, once a person learns of the unconscious and how to work with it, they can begin to have more conscious input into the flow of their life.

The related and equally unhelpful attitude that can result from holding individuals to be consciously responsible for their reality is a total disregard for social justice. Success and its resulting financial and political power, no matter what the means used to achieve it, is taken as a personal victory, the mark of the superior, more highly evolved, and more spiritually blessed or enlightened person. Calvinism especially enshrined this point of view, looking upon material prosperity as a mark of being among the elect or the saved. This gave the green light to the wealthy to excel at profit making and to acquire more and more. It is one of the underpinning dogmas of capitalism.

The 'truth' that we create our own reality needs to be balanced by the deep compassion of the psyche functioning in an awareness of being at one with all that is. Only when we can experientially get that whatever we do to anyone or anything else we also do to ourselves ('what goes around, comes around'), have we truly matured at a spiritual level.

Anything less than universal compassion indicates that we are creating a reality that is still limited and shaped by our fear.

A further difficulty within the esoteric tradition is its cosmological model. It holds that the universe happened when the One or Mind came out from itself and started to cascade downwards. The reasons why this happened at all are not really clear. It is known as emanationism, because to emanate is to shine forth or to come out of something. Mind was seen to be totally coherent light, so that in it everything was as it should be. Mind was one in itself.

When it started to pour out or come forth, however, the energy was seen to be decreasing. This was judged as things getting worse. The resulting entities were given names, identified with a hierarchy of spiritual beings: cherubim, seraphim, thrones, powers, principalities, dominations, and archangels (see Paul, in his letters to the Colossians 1:16 and Ephesians 1:21; 6:12). These energies were considered to be part of Mind, but each just a bit lesser than it. Within a Gnostic pantheon, they would be the first-born from the Godhead. As you get further from Mind, there is less and less clarity and more illusion. The stars and the planets are considered an intermediary realm, and form a bridge by which one might access the higher realms, thus the Gnostic interest in astrology. By the time you get to earth and material reality, things are very dark and dense. The Gnostics also said that the true God was Mind, and that Yahweh was just one of the lesser powers. Because he was not always a nice guy, they said he couldn't be the supreme being.

The serious problem with this model is that it has generally led to dualism: the notion that spirit is good and matter is bad. Men have identified themselves with spirit/intellect, and seen women as the means by which spirit, or souls, are trapped in matter through birth. When it suited them, men dissociated themselves from being the sole source of human life (see Apollo, p. 70 above), and held women as the culprits for the evil of a soul being born into the world (see Genesis 3:12–13).

On the other hand, the benefit of being aware that I am creating my own reality is that it gives me some understanding of what my issues are and so offers more effective options for making choices. In a world of uncertainty and seemingly random chaos, being aware that my inner fear and conflicts contribute to what I encounter from one day to the next gives me the option of taking steps to ease the fear and conflict, so as to have some input into the flow of my life. This is the basis of all true empowerment. An example might be someone who finds themselves constantly disregarded by others. They could consider the possibility that their self-esteem is low; in other words, they don't think they are worth being taken seriously. I have often seen people who start to have more regard for themselves being given more respect by other people in their lives. It leads to more assertive behaviour, thus prompting a change in response from those around them.

The problems at the heart of the difficulty with knowing that a person creates their own reality are those of suffering and death. The rational mind prefers to avoid suffering at all costs and sees it only as a bad thing, bad in both senses of the word: unpleasant *and* a sign of punishment for moral culpability. This is another one of those knife-edges of balance. Suffering is not something to be pursued and yet neither is it something which is either entirely avoidable or without use. Suffering is the concrete manifestation of the fear that is the hallmark of rational consciousness.

The Buddhist response to suffering has been to advise detachment. If we can stop fighting against suffering it becomes merely pain. It is explained as being the result of bad karma, something that is to be endured in order either to pay a debt or to learn what not to do again. The difficulty with the admonition not to fight against suffering is that it can deteriorate into passive resignation.

The Christian approach to suffering, that it is punishment for sins, is even more unhelpful. Jesus is said to have taken on the suffering due to human sin. Following this line of thought, overzealous saints have entered into a masochistic pursuit of suffering to 'help redeem the world'. Even more reprehensible has been the approach to children which says that they must suffer for their misbehaviour. This has exacerbated the level of fear in people, causing untold damage to millions of children in fervently Christian countries. Again, this approach is part of the package of a judging and vengeful god who dominates and intimidates his followers with threats of everlasting suffering. Yet it is also understandable as anyone who has suffered can all too easily feel that someone has a vendetta against him or her. What did I do to deserve this?

More recently, the insight that suffering is pain that is resisted has been combined with the practice of mindfulness. This is the letting go of resistance to the pain in tandem with a simple awareness of the present moment. It is the most effective pain relief available. This is not a passive resignation to pain, nor a pursuit of 'salvific' pain, but a simple 'being with' pain, which makes it tolerable. Mindfulness can also be practised as a path to spiritual enlightenment, leading to the awareness of being one with all that is. This allows a person to take a very unpleasant experience and make it a path to spiritual liberation. This, however, is not a part of the original Buddhist understanding.

On the other hand, a mindful approach to pain is not one of passive acceptance of oppression that is caused by society or cruel or thoughtless people in one's environment. Pain that is avoidable should be relieved because there is more than enough of the unavoidable with which to practise. Chronic physical pain is caused by untreated, long-term trauma. It can and should be relieved by techniques recently developed (see P. Levine and M. Phillips' *Freedom from Pain,* 2012).

A materialist spirituality, as exemplified in the ideal life according to the American way that expects no pain and all gain, is the one most at a loss for understanding suffering in a value-neutral way. The American consumerist model defines the maximization of pleasure and the elimination of all pain, or even inconvenience, as the ideal state of human existence. The pharmaceutical industry, as a stalwart representative of the materialist/consumerist world, sells a plethora of pills for you to pop to eliminate your pain.

The New Age approach has often been combined with the materialist ideal, when it suggests that if a person does the 'right' spiritual practice faithfully they will be spared all pain, suffering, and an early death. But if one examines the healthiest of the New Age perspectives more closely, one finds that its wisdom indicates that we are here to grow and deepen in our understanding of love and power. If our fear has shaped our thinking or emotional reality into a self-destructive pattern then often the process of reshaping and healing ourselves emotionally will involve an experience of pain. Thus, if you have become codependent on an abusive partner or friend because your mother was emotionally unavailable, then you need to leave such a relationship and learn how to love yourself first before engaging with others.

The common experience that change is painful for us is due to the rigidity with which we hang onto our perceptions of how things are. Fear makes us rigid. Not until we realize that the rigidity is more painful than the insecurity involved in trusting that all will be well, will we be freed from the worst of our pain. The parallel questions of 'when do we push for a solution to our pain?' and 'when do we simply accept things as they are, so that we can expand our being to accommodate them?' can only be dealt with by going deeply within, and listening to the still, small voice. The individual needs the ability to look at the reality in which they find themselves, and to try to discern what lesson life seems to be posing. It is the wisdom advised by the Serenity Prayer: Grant me the serenity to accept the things I cannot change, the courage to change the things I can, and the wisdom to know the difference (Reinhold Niebuhr).

One of the ways of going within which has been lost to Western consciousness due to the vilification of the flesh is the act of entering into the body's experience. This is not the obsession with beauty and youthfulness pressed on us by a consumerist society, but a sitting with all the communications of the body for which we generally don't take time.

In Western tradition women have been taught that their bodies are primarily for enticing sexual partners, while men have been trained to be tough and indifferent to their bodies (unless instructed otherwise by the fashion, cosmetics, and sports industries). Shifting to loving your body and experiencing the power of its creativity in more than sexual ways can eventually bring you to an experience of your divinity and your ability to create your own reality. From a contemporary understanding of the soul level, we create our reality primarily so that we may grow and heal, not simply so that we can avoid pain.

However, the creation of reality also needs to be addressed at the collective level. People impact on each other, no matter how withdrawn or isolated one may seek to be. Systems at every level join us together and make our every thought and action part of a vast web which compromises the extent to which we can exercise free choice. This has been captured in the recent image from chaos theory of the impact that the fluttering of a butterfly's wings can have on weather at the other side of the planet (see chaos theory).

Once again, however, this brings us to the door of a very difficult balancing act: how do we allow people individual freedom while at the same time ensuring the common good? The religion of capitalism has made the individual's freedom sacrosanct while the religion of communism has failed in its promise to ensure the greatest good for the most people.

As the plane door opened that September of 1977 at the airport in Lagos, Nigeria I was flooded with a riptide of sensations. First there was the moistness of the air, lush, sweet smelling, with an undercurrent of the less savoury end of our olfactory range. The light was brilliant, intense, and the heat immediately started to drill into my bones. But even more than the sensual rush, there was a sudden awareness of a world whose way of experiencing reality was very different from anything I had ever known. It was scary and beguiling at the same time. The only way I had of articulating this at the time was as an example of Teilhard de Chardin's noosphere – the layer of human thinking that envelops the earth in a similar way to the air of our atmosphere.

Stairs wheeled to the plane's side and out we poured, making landfall on the African continent. It had been drummed into me by those with many years of life in Africa – DON'T DRINK THE WATER! Westerners haven't developed a tolerance for the plethora of microbial life that most West Africans have acquired to survive childhood. In the heat, I was suddenly thirsty and bought a glass of squash – a fruit concentrate mixed with ... oh my god! Immediately after I had gulped down the glass I was quickly hit with an awareness of my folly. I could see this was going to be a challenging adjustment.

Eventually, I connected with the friends who had come to pick me up. The last leg of this several-day journey was by car on a long, bumpy, unpaved bush road in the back of a Volkswagen Beetle. By the time we arrived at our destination, a medical compound deep in the centre of Nigeria, I was thoroughly disoriented. I knew that gravity still seemed to be pulling down, but everything else was up for grabs! This included the contents of my stomach, which decided to defy gravity.

After a month or two in Nigeria, I wrote the following entries in my journal:

October 11 1977

It is only when you move out of alignment with the patterns of your surroundings that you can see between the lines. And behold! God fills the universe. He is in between the lines, round and throughout, ever present and intimately woven into reality. If you are focused on the lines, you can't see between them.

October 16

This indeed seems to be the place where I am called. It ain't easy but it pulls every fibre in my being to vibrate with the deepest currents of life.

November 28

Caught between two worlds, each its own reality. Where do I live? My heart – where is my heart? Fired by the greater Reality, love is the seasoning for so much else – loneliness, culture shock, tiredness. Where am I and what am I looking for? What a madness it is to love, and yet that is what I am all about. But the madness carries me in desperate humours.

Thus began a profound overhaul of my entire being. It was a refiner's fire that repeatedly stripped me to my core and insisted that I reconsider everything I had ever known to be true.

Chapter 7

Becoming Aware of Our Divinity

God became human in order that humans could become divine.

Irenaeus (c. 130–202 CE)

In Chapter 2, I gave a brief description of how I came to my own awareness that 'I am God as Jesus was God'. At the time, this was a very worrisome development for me, because I was also aware of the megalomaniac inflation which has been visited on those who have seen themselves as equal to God. So it was in fear and trembling, to borrow Kierkegaard's phrase, that I gingerly proceeded to hold this hypothesis while continuing on my spiritual explorations. As indicated above, it has required me to clarify what I mean by 'god', and also to look at who Jesus was.

Jesus himself seems to have gained the awareness of his oneness with all that is, as manifested in his saying that 'whatever you do to the least of these, you do to me' (Matthew 25:45). In a number of mystical traditions, such as Hinduism, Hermeticism, and Mahayana Buddhism, realizing that you are one with all that is, is taken as the mark of an enlightened being. The Jewish tradition in the first century, however, had no such concept. For them, there was only the human being, refugee from the Garden of Eden, and Yahweh with his messengers (*angelos* in Greek). The prophets were seen as being closer to Yahweh because of their knowledge of the Word of the Lord. This is also consistent with the dualism which had shaped Jewish religious expression while it was in Babylon.

When Job challenged Yahweh's obvious unfairness he was subdued with a splash of splendour. In Job 38–39 Yahweh boasts of his powerful acts but never actually addresses his unfairness. Unjust rulers have continued to make use of similar tactics down through the ages. Job, having been written after the Jews returned from exile in Babylon, reflects an image of a god lording it over humans. With the pre-exilic prophets such as Isaiah and Hosea, however, there was an understanding of Yahweh as compassionate to the downtrodden and the poor.

The common corollaries of being enlightened have been a sense of compassion for all other living beings and the ability to work miracles, that is, to do things not generally possible for other humans. Similarly, these are traits of Jesus described in the Christian Testament. It would have been from this sense of compassion that Jesus would have opposed both the judging and punishing perpetrated by the religious authorities of his time, and the economic and social exploitation by the Roman businessmen of the people in Palestine.

Since Jewish thought did not allow the notion of a divine human being, the writers of the Gospels of Matthew, Mark, and Luke used the tradition of an expected saviour to talk about who Jesus was. The precise characteristics of this saviour varied according to which faction within Jewish Palestine, or the diaspora (those Jews still living in other countries), with whom one would have spoken. There were those who saw him as a political liberator, fulfilling the promise Yahweh had made to David to keep Israel a free country (2 Samuel 7:8–17). Others saw him as a prophet of Wisdom who would enforce social justice and equality in the face of oppression and injustice (see E. Schüssler Fiorenza's *Miriam's Child, Sophia's Prophet,* 2015).

When the phrase 'Son of God' is used in the Bible, its meaning is that of a paradigmatic or archetypal human being. This is also the meaning of the phrase 'Son of Man' which comes from the Book of Daniel. This book was written in the apocalyptic times, that is, the centuries after the Jews returned to Palestine from their sojourn in Babylon until the destruction of Jerusalem in 64 CE by the Romans. To read these titles as indicators of divinity in the Messiah is to impose a modern mindset on the Jewish frame of reference. For Jews of that time, such an idea would have been considered blasphemous.

In addition, Judaism has the tradition of a scapegoat who was sacrificed by a priest to appease Yahweh's anger at the sins of the Jews. This, then, became another layer of interpretation, or construction, of the identity of Jesus. He was seen as both the sacrificial victim *and* the priestly sacrificer (Letter to the Hebrews). Anointing was the ritual in Judaism which was used to confer special status on their kings and high priests. In Hebrew the word for 'anointed one' is *messiah*. In Greek the word for the 'anointed one' is *christ*, which is how Jesus got his surname.

The Greeks did have a tradition of a divine human being and John's Gospel made use of this idea to describe who Jesus was. The understanding of divinity found in Greek religion is of a superior being who is immortal, but who nonetheless suffers many of the psychological/emotional foibles of ordinary humans. However, combining the Greek tradition of a divine man with the Jewish notion of the divine – which is of an almighty, omniscient, and judging entity – led to a more potent divine man. Later, further additions of Greek philosophical concepts from Plato and Aristotle, such as the highest good, and the Hermetical picture of Absolute Mind to this mix, produced a quantum leap in the understanding of divinity which fuelled the Christian religion.

For centuries after the divinity of Jesus had been decided on as gospel truth various groups of Christians argued and fought over just exactly what this meant. Many of the early councils of the Christian Church were held to try to determine exactly how Jesus was 'truly God and truly man'. These early debates in the Christian churches were a mix of politically motivated power grabbing and theological wrestling. Phrasings, down to the smallest nuance, were honed and explored. For example, was Jesus' divinity *like* that of the Father, or *exactly the same as*? This turned, literally, on a few letters in a word, *ópoiov* as opposed to *ópooúʋiov* (homoion vs homoousion). Often, the humanity of Jesus was totally lost in the shuffle. Yet the doctrine was there, awaiting further pondering.

The understanding of divinity

The issue now is do we accept an understanding of divinity, or a divine human and his role in history, which is based in the national consciousness of one Middle Eastern ethnic group? Why should one particular group's historically conditioned self-articulation become the standard for our view of the divine for the rest of human history? This sort of absolutizing mindset is characteristic of rational consciousness before it has become self-aware and self-reflecting. For those who have stepped out of this box, the answer is an obvious no. Yet for those who still base their spirituality on this particular story, moving out of that box is seen as a betrayal of the divine.

When I was working as a missionary in Ghana, it became more obvious to me that the Christian Scriptures were the early community's efforts to communicate their experience of an impressive person, using the traditional religion of the Jews. My challenge to Ghanaians in my *Bible Reading Guide for Ghana* was to ask them to use their traditional religion to say who Jesus was. Because Christianity has been the dominant point of view on the nature of the divine in the West for so many centuries, and also because it states that its view can be the only true one, people find it difficult to consider the possibility of other ways of understanding what might constitute the divine or an enlightened human being.

When someone challenges the status quo, they generally take one of two routes: they deny that the divine exists or they accept the picture of the divine offered in another religion or philosophy. The former option is unhelpful because, as observed earlier, we need the marker of the divine to keep us from being reduced to what is already manifested. We need a projective screen upon which to foresee our future possibilities.

In particular, the image of a divine saviour fulfilled a specific role in the evolution of human consciousness. It promoted a focus on the individual, which brought human consciousness to a place where self-awareness and self-reflection could be highly developed (see Larry Siedentop's *Inventing the Individual, 2014*). This in turn has enabled rational consciousness to relate to intuitive consciousness in a balanced and creative manner rather than being overwhelmed by the rational mind's underlying fear. While this growth in consciousness was slowly manifesting, the idea of there being a saviour helped us to cope with a god who pronounced our projected self-condemnation.

Yet the latter option, of seeing the 'real truth' in exotic places, is also fraught with difficulties because all religions have arisen from within very specific historical contexts. The details of their beliefs and rituals are limited by their context. This is not to say that religions don't contain wisdom that is still pertinent for us today. But the difficulty of 'old wine skins' is one that Jesus flagged a long time ago. As we move forward in our evolution of consciousness we need new images and symbols for that which transcends us individually and collectively.

The role played by the many avatars, or human manifestations of a god or goddess, in other religions, especially Hinduism, is an example of an image of the divine which is not connected to being human. The avatars have generally come to reveal some truth to humanity, or simply to inspire devotion. There is no inherent value in the humanity of these beings. Despite the fact that Jesus' humanity was very much neglected, except for its gruesome suffering, during most of the two millennia of its history, it was never abandoned. Whatever the reasons for this, it has been a crucial piece of balance in an otherwise dualistic picture. The non-valuing of the body in Hindu avatars and divine men and women in Greek and Roman stories is a significant flaw in their spiritual health.

Now, as we have begun to leave behind the image of divinity which has been held until recently, it is important to look at what characteristics we do want to ascribe to the divine. Further, and even more importantly, how do we access our own divinity and what does that mean in our day-to-day living? In my opinion, the message within the Christian Scriptures which is most life-giving and most creative is that 'God [the divine] is love'. All the other details and parts of that story, which talk of judgement and punishment on the part of the divine, or on the 'Will of God', I would suggest, do not square up with this central theme within the story of Jesus.

For Jesus, the 'law of love' is 'do unto others what you would have them do to you' (Luke 6:31). Matthew 7:12 goes even further: 'So in everything, do to others what you would have them do to you, for this sums up the Law and the Prophets.' Here, Jesus is quoted as specifically equating his entire religious tradition with this simple golden rule. This is not an idea entirely original to him, as there are versions of it starting in ancient Babylon and Egypt which were further developed by the Greeks. It is more commonly called the law of reciprocity, and evolved through several forms: starting with a recommendation not to ('you shouldn't do what you don't want done to you'), on to a definite prohibition ('don't do'), then edging onto a positive suggestion ('you should do to others what you would like done to you'). Jesus would appear to be the first to make it a definite 'do'!

Interestingly, developmental psychology has also identified love as the most important experience within the human repertoire for the promotion of growth and human maturity (see T. Lewis et al.'s *A General Theory of Love,* 2001). It is on the basis of this agreement between Jesus and psychology, as well as my own intuitive sense of rightness about it, that I have arrived at the focus on love (or compassion) as being the primary guideline for assessing the health of a spirituality. The promotion of true self-love ('love others as you love yourself', Mark 12:31), a sense that each of us is loveable, and the easing of our fear are basic characteristics of a healthy sense of the divine.

The danger of inflation or megalomania is a notable pitfall in recommending that people get in touch with their divinity. Contemporary advertising already panders to our narcissism by telling us that we're worth it or deserve things, when its only purpose is to make money for advertisers. In addition, the era of the 'white man's burden' promoted many forms of bigotry, including racism and sexism. That is why the characteristics of compassion, social justice, and ecology are crucial requirements within a framework looking to craft a *psychologically healthy* spirituality.

Non-dualism

A further reflection on the divine is that it is *our* divinity, in the sense that everything that exists participates equally in the divine. Each of us is part of the divine, and no one individual is more divine than any other. This includes animals and things as well as other human beings. No matter how enlightened a person is, or appears, they are no more divine than you or me or the rock. Thus divinity functions in a holographic manner. The whole is visible in the part.

The important function of this last conviction is that it eliminates any dualistic propensities in human thinking. When everything is seen to be composed of the same energy, then there can be no disparaging of some people or the material world. All must be treated with respect (thus social justice and ecology) since we all rise from the same energy.

The greatest challenge to this conviction is the obvious differences between humans and the rest of the world. The privileging of human consciousness started with the rise of *rational* consciousness. Intuitive consciousness has historically been well able to perceive non-human consciousness, as any familiarity with shamanic experience or other 'primitive' animism demonstrates. But since the Age of Enlightenment the existence of this huge part of the universe was disappeared by a left-brain-dominant culture.

The only real difference between human consciousness and the consciousness found in all that makes up nature is that only humans have free will. Free will gives us the option to choose to be out of balance, whereas nature consciousnesses, for example animals or plants, do not have this option. Nature is always inherently in balance with all that is (see M. S. Wright and her writings from Perelandra). Human beings have caused imbalance in nature, which then has taken steps to rebalance itself. Evolution in nature also leads to change where what has been disappears and new expressions of life take their turn. But it is not a fear-engendering process for nature.

The other dualistic practice of judging some people to be good and others to be bad, in a moral sense, has allowed the physically powerful to use this splitting device to justify their aggression against others. Rather, it is important to respect each person's uniqueness while at the same time balancing individual needs and gifts with the good of the collective. Differences in stages of psychological and physical development are a much more useful, and morally neutral, demarcation among individuals. Ken Wilber's strategy in this regard is one of the best I have seen for understanding development in a spectrum paradigm rather than a hierarchical one. This means that there is a direction of development from less developed to more developed but not a sense of inherent goodness or superiority in an above and below way. For example, an adult is not morally superior to a child or deserving of more respect even though they are capable of more morally nuanced actions. (See K. Wilbur's *The Eye of Spirit*, 2001).

The irrational/non-rational

What we identify as the characteristics of the divine will depend to a great extent on how we understand the qualities of energy which transcend the generally perceived world. Quantum physicists disagree among themselves as to what this is. There are three main theories about how energy and reality function. In each instance the role of consciousness is central.

In the theory accepted by 70 per cent of these physicists (see A. Bruce's *Beyond the Bleep*, 2005), every possible event is actually occurring simultaneously in parallel universes (the 'many worlds interpretation'). But our consciousness can only see this one. Another suggestion is that there is a constant superposition of all possibilities hovering, but that when consciousness observes, there is a 'wave function collapse'. This means that just one of those infinite possibilities becomes real. The third opinion is that consciousness and its 'quantum gravity' is itself this 'wave function collapse'.

As you can see, the translation of abstract mathematical equations into a story of reality is not a scientific affair. It is done through the lens of the consciousness of the individual scientist. But what does come through in each of the attempts to explain reality from a quantum physics point of view is that there is a lot more going on in the universe than we are, or can be, aware of rationally.

Obviously, these theories move beyond what is sensible to the rational mind. But then mathematics has always been noteworthy for its ability to boggle the rational mind. It blithely speaks of multiple universes, non-Euclidian geometries, and more than a few systems of logic.

There is also the nifty invention of imaginary numbers, which are created when the quantity $\sqrt{-1}$, generally represented by *i*, is used. Obviously, no negative number multiplied by itself will give a negative number (a negative times a negative is always a positive). Yet this irrationality is essential for calculating the behaviour of electricity, usually described as the flow of electrons.

These examples help to demonstrate that the world is much bigger than what we experience or can even conceive of. So when some people prefer to speak in terms of parallel realities, or multiple lifetimes, or non-human conscious beings, this isn't all that different from what mathematicians do. It is only the bias held by scientists against intuitive irrationalities that makes such a distinction.

The crucial consideration in the non-rational aspects of one's sense of the divine is that they not violate the law of love, that is, they need to increase love, decrease fear, and promote social justice and ecology. Those parts of a spirituality that are produced by intuition need to be held accountable to these guidelines because intuition is not infallible.

It is the quality of human existence, which is promoted by one's sense of the divine, that is the point at which you discern the health of a spirituality.

If you hold spiritual beliefs which promote fear on any level, individual or systemic, then you are promoting ill health.

The one and the many

One of the greatest difficulties which the early Christian Church had in articulating the divinity of Jesus was in figuring out how to harness it to his humanity without distorting either of them. Interestingly, this difficulty is still with us. If we are one with all that is, then how can we at the same time each be a separate entity, with a free will and unique identity? Some people reject the notion of monism on this very point. How can there be only one underlying energy in the universe without reducing us all to mere clones of the universal Mind?

This brings us back to yet another very early philosophical problem:

the one and the many. Is there only a Oneness which expresses itself in infinite ways but all of which will ultimately fall back into this One? How can I truly be an individual, worthy of respect and accommodation in the world, if all separation is only an illusion? Yet if there are Two, then a seemingly endless power struggle ensues to determine which is the Good and which the Bad, which the more powerful, which the more privileged, which came first.

I would suggest that both Oneness and Twoness are necessary concepts in our understanding of reality if we are to function well. It's similar to the wave/particle problem in physics. Light (as well as other particles) behaves as both a wave and a particle. It is a fundamental uncertainty in reality as science apprehends it. Perhaps it is simply that our minds as they function at this level of reality are incapable of seeing what's going on. The book *Flatland* (Abbott, 1884), written over a hundred years ago, does an excellent job of conveying the problem through the conversation between a two-dimensional square and a three-dimensional sphere. The sphere can see things from a perspective not possible to the square.

Edges of the known world

Psychology has given us much new information and insight into what it means to be human. Yet any good psychology will not exceed its remit and attempt to talk about spirit. However, Carl Jung used the notion of archetypes in his analytical psychology. These are organizing principles that exist independently of any specific examples of any one of them. They take us one step away from concrete reality and into the quantum physical world of potentialities.

Everything that exists is said to have an archetypal field that organizes its existence. Common examples would be the ideal or general notion of mother, father, child, the divine, beauty, etc. Jung made use of the idea of archetypes because of the repetition of specific patterns across many different informational sources. This would include dreams from individuals greatly separated in time and space, fairy tales from different cultures, and information emerging from the new field of quantum physics.

Jung was fortunate to be involved in an ongoing conversation with the quantum physicist Wolfgang Pauli. In this way he was kept abreast of the latest thinking about field theory. A field is something that organizes things and events which exist in it, in the same way that a magnetic field organizes iron filings into a characteristic pattern. At the quantum level, things happen in a way not limited by the laws of time and space. Acausality, where two things happen at the same time but one doesn't directly *cause* the other, is an example of this. Acausality fits well with the way in which archetypes can be felt behind synchronistic experiences (see S. Gieser's *The Innermost Kernel,* 2005). Most people have met or heard of someone who has incredibly bad luck, who always seems to end up being a victim, or someone who always seems to have money. Each of them functions under the influence of an energy which seems to haunt or enhance their life but for which there is no obvious immediate cause.

In this way, science, in its quantum physics expression, is beginning to talk about reality more as a magical place than as one limited by the laws of time and space as we have known it. But rather than this being caused by a god or spirits, it is understood to be simply the nature of energy and how it interacts with consciousness. A lot of what used to be considered the realm of the divine no longer needs that construct to explain it. So what might the divine look like in a contemporary version?

Emerging spiritualities

While there are full-blown religions which have emerged in the past few hundred years (see S. Moncrieff's *God: A User's Guide*, 2006), I will confine myself to what are generally referred to as New Age religions or spiritualities. This is a huge field with more variety than is commonly realized. There is a very good review of, and reflection on, most of the New Age genre to be found in a tome by the name of *New Age Religion and Western Culture: Esotericism in the Mirror of Secular Thought* by W. J. Hanegraaff (1997). He analyses New Age phenomena from many relevant angles and most of his conclusions I would agree with. Unfortunately he comes at it from a strictly academic and apparently theist frame of reference. This means he seems unable to grasp significant psychological realities from an experiential perspective. He also insists on inserting a god into some of the sources which do not really make use of this notion. Nevertheless, Hanegraaff has done a massive amount of work with a comprehensive grasp of esoteric sources and his work is a gift for those who wish to gain an in-depth perspective on the New Age. I am indebted to him for my overview.

There are emerging descriptions of spirit and bigger pictures, or cosmologies, announced by various New Age authors. These are generally communicated by channelled sources, with the notable exception of Michael Newton's research which uses hypnosis. Channelling is the same mode of perception that has given us revelations of all sorts, inspired writings or scriptures throughout history. Whether you understand it as coming from a separate entity, superior or not, or as the product of our accessing the collective unconscious or the Akashic records doesn't make that much difference. It is information that is not arrived at through the use of logical reasoning, deduction, or the scientific method. What does matter are the implications of what is described.

Hanegraaff notes that one overwhelming consensus within the New Age perspective is a positive attitude towards this world, apart from the *Course in Miracles* (Schucman, 1976). (This work, in keeping with its purported Christian source, sees this world as a valley of tears and suffering.) This pro-world attitude is the result of the New Age's conscious interest in restoring balance from the anti-worldly nature of monotheistic religions which are dualistic. Even when the New Age perspective concurs with the notion of maya, it sees it as an important and useful illusion in the overall project of being human.

Quite a few of the more popular or commonly known New Age approaches, however, speak from a place which assumes that they 'know the truth'. And even when they don't present themselves with this air people tend to hear them as authority figures. Sources such as Seth, Ramtha, Abraham, among a great many others, can then be followed as gods in their own right and anyone who isn't on board with their revelation isn't as enlightened or cool. Their channellers can also take or be given exalted status (and a lot of money). Gurus also partake in this dynamic by providing salvation for people who haven't been educated to take responsibility for themselves and how they make meaning of their lives.

On the other hand, reality is a social affair and it is very difficult to maintain a vision of reality that isn't reinforced by at least some of the people we associate with. This is what makes these times particularly difficult, as there are not always likeminded souls in our immediate geographical vicinity. The internet has more recently helped relieve this situation, with its worldwide reach.

Interestingly enough, the New Age sources which I have found myself drawn to are not any of those reviewed in Hanegraaff's book. For whatever reason, those authors whose stories I found more plausible are ones who have not made as big a splash in the general New Age scene. They are Patrick Francis McMahon's *The Grand Design* (1987–1996), as well as his other three titles presenting his discussions with Krishnamurti and Margaret Anna Cusack; Machaelle S. Wright and her books, *Behaving As If the God in All Life Matters* (1987), *The Garden Workbook I* (1993), *Dancing in the Shadows of the Moon* (1995) among others written at her nature research centre in Virginia, Perelandra; and Michael Newton's *Journey of Souls (1994), Destiny of Souls (2000)*, and *Life between Lives (2004)*.

None of these three authors speaks in terms of a god. McMahon, or rather his spirit guide Shebaka, uses the term 'God' but is clear that this is primarily for the comfort of his readers. 'God is not a person ... each of us being a part of God ... God is an infinity of spirit existing through infinity.' (*The Grand Design, Vol. 1*, p. 31.) He also speaks about the importance of each of us recognizing that we are God. For Wright, the only big spiritual guns she mentions are a group of spirit guides known through history as the White Brotherhood (where 'white' means full spectrum energy, not men in white hoods; and 'brotherhood' means family; you are free to rename them once you let them know what term you will use). She identifies Devas, a term referring to archetypal consciousnesses, and Pan who is the 'CEO' of nature spirits. Newton specifically questioned his participants about anything resembling what is commonly understood as God, but none of them had encountered any hint of such an entity.

Thus, the healthiest contemporary spiritualities, from my point of view, have a cosmology rather than a theology. These three authors describe the whatness of all that is. They all make use of the contemporary story of the Big Bang to conceive of the initiation of reality with an appropriately fuzzy sense of what preceded this explosion. It started an evolutionary process involving different types of consciousness (not just human), whose overall mission is the decrease of fear and the increase of love. There are multiple dimensions; it is infinite, that is, beyond the conceiving of our minds. There is no personal god, but there is a sense of the divine – something big, beyond us as individuals, yet of which we are a part.

McMahon has all souls come into being at the Big Bang. Wright describes the same thing, but distinguishes between Soul and souls. Individual souls came into being with the Big Bang, but Soul pre-existed it. Newton's sources saw souls coming into being from a wall of pulsating light. This allows for the notion of older and younger souls in his cosmology.

The source of fear in souls is described in *The Grand Design* as being the free choice of only one per cent of all souls to give away their personal power to other souls whom they saw as more impressive. It is obviously a symbolic story, trying to identify loss of self-esteem as the source of all fear. Newton's sources offer the view that fear happens when new souls are confronted with the vulnerability of being in an earth-type body. Their spiritual growth involves the gradual shedding of this fear while becoming wiser in their interaction with other souls. Wright doesn't address the problem of the source of fear.

Most contemporary spiritualities make use of the notion of multiple lifetimes, often taking place simultaneously across many dimensions and universes. This greatly expands on the Christian assertion that we have only one lifetime and if we make a serious mess of it, we will spend eternity in hell. This expansion eliminates the power of anyone to instil fear into us by threatening us with judgement (which is probably why this nearly universal concept has been ignored or rejected by any authority-driven religion). With a bigger picture, there is time and space to keep working at learning to love ourselves and others. Some who are conditioned to the single lifetime approach may feel a bit dizzy when they are exposed to a story with a much larger sense of how big this whole project is, but that stretching is no harm.

The objection that we would remember if we had been in other lifetimes has been shown to be unsustainable. There is a lot of evidence that some people do remember other lifetimes, with some fairly dramatic stories having been published over the years. For example, see J. Cockell's *Yesterday's Children* (1993), S. Lucas, *Past Life Dreamwork* (2008), and *Soul Survivor* by B. and A. Leininger (2010). In all of these instances, it was possible for the person to go back and either actually make contact with people who knew the person when in their other lifetime, or for historical documentation to confirm facts first posited by past life reports. Otherwise, not remembering allows us to respond from deep within ourselves to the current circumstances. These are seen to be set by our self, at a soul level, to provide another opportunity for learning to love ourselves and others.

The people of Nigeria, Cameroon, Ghana – more precisely, Ibos and Igalas, the people of Bamenda, and Brong-Ahafo Akans – sank deep roots into my heart, and shared the reality of their lives. It was a reality rich in human connections, but also in connections with the spirit world. During the space between my life in Cameroon and Ghana, spent in Kansas City, Missouri, I read Laurens van der Post's *The Lost World of the Kalahari*. I had noted the passage where his filming equipment wouldn't function in the sacred place of the Bushmen. Later, when I was in the Twi language school at the beginning of my stay in Ghana, we visited the compound of a local spirit healer. I had my camera with me, and took a few photos. The camera seemed to work without difficulty. Yet when the film was developed, these were the only pictures that were simply blank. That camera did not have a lens cover, it being an Instamatic! Someone else I knew also visited that compound and had the same experience with her camera. Reality is not as simple as science would have us believe.

The upshot of my African adventures and relationships was that I found myself having to consider my position.

> *February 12 1985 [Sunyani, Ghana]*
>
> Before, even though I was aware of being different from many others in the community, I enjoyed my work and there was nothing else I wanted to do. Perhaps it has been my exposure to [the thought of Carl] Jung that has helped me to come to see that now there is something else I want to do. I need to be with people who are grappling with God along the same lines that I am finding myself drawn [to]. To be with them in order to tease out my own thinking and expression, to clarify and be challenged by others who want to move in the same direction – so that there will be exchange and not defense. I also want to celebrate God in ways that express how I have come to know him, and that is different to the traditional Mass with its priests and 'God out there'!

I had moved to Boston, MA by the beginning of 1986. One of the first things I did after getting a place to live and a job was to get in touch with Rosemary Haughton at her shelter for homeless women north of Boston. I had read Rosemary's book, *The Passionate God*, while I had been in Cameroon, and found it tremendously inspiring. She and her community celebrated their Eucharistic liturgy without the aid of an ordained minister. This was exactly what I was looking for. It was fortuitous that I had found what I was looking for so quickly, because within a year's time, I realized that the entire Christian frame of reference with regard to the divine no longer spoke to me. I woke up one morning and suddenly realized that I was no longer a Christian.

> April 20 1987
>
> Just so much has happened since last I wrote. I hardly recognize myself, especially with regard to God talk. I've lost it all, yet I don't miss it because something deeper has come in its place. There is nothing 'out there' to talk about. All is within, and I am within all. The task is to explore myself and let that be.
>
> Suppose I should also mention other details like having left

> Ghana, having had the knee op, having left MSHR [Missionary Sisters of the Holy Rosary], 'making it in Massachusetts!', having lost all sense of direction. What will I be when I grow up? Skimming through this book I am impressed by my own experiences and articulation. So where the hell am I going? What will become of me? Surely there is too much here just to have it evaporate into the night. 'Sometimes I feel like a motherless child ...'

When I am speaking to people about having been a missionary in West Africa, to avoid them jumping to a host of inaccurate assumptions, I finish with the comment that 'they converted me – an occupational hazard!' A close friend who had been in Ghana with me, and who remained in the community until her death, observed, 'Yes, that's exactly what happened!' And so it is.

Chapter 8

Getting to Our Divinity

Before enlightenment, chop wood, carry water.
After enlightenment, chop wood, carry water.

Zen proverb

I return again to the brief description, which I gave in Chapter 2, of how I came to my own awareness that I am God as Jesus was God. It involved emotional, intellectual, and spiritual developments, and would not have been possible without all three of these aspects interweaving and working together. These conditions had been interactive in my being and so produced what seemed a sudden awakening. In reality, it was a slow process which gradually prepared me to consider such a troubling and profound possibility. I will look at each of these developmental aspects in my own being, and then you can consider how other spiritual paths might make something similar possible for you.

Emotional

My emotional development had been severely impacted by both my parents' own emotional difficulties and then by the ensuing peer rejection which further challenged my accessing a satisfactory sense of self. The first 18 years of my life were difficult and painful emotionally. I had coped by retreating into my intellect, which, as a thinking type, was relatively congenial to me. I also spent a lot of time in nature, the only solace available, my brothers and I having been intentionally isolated from the rest of society by my parents. College had been a breath of fresh air because there I found peers who also functioned primarily from their intellect. Finally I was 'normal'!

But the internal pain of the previous 18 years wasn't to be shrugged off quite so blithely. Despite being among similarly functioning folks I began to experience significant bouts of depression each January/ February. Fortunately, I had begun working with a counsellor and this had set in motion a process of emotional healing that eventually made self-acceptance possible. It is only if we have been affirmed, loved, mirrored, and relieved of judgement that we are able to truly love our self and to recognize our own divinity. This is fundamentally what a good psychotherapist should provide to the person who attends them.

More recently, how this works has been explored in the phenomenon called 'mirroring'. It happens when a person responds in a like manner to what they experience in a person on whom they are focused. Postures tend to come into sync, as well as their breathing; this does not happen consciously, but in a manner that is amazing and affirming. This is the basis for quite a few human behaviours and traits, such as imitation, language learning, skill learning, social attunement, empathy, and self-awareness. It happens initially before the age of one year, and is crucial in terms of both social and self-development. If we are not adequately mirrored our ability to understand the emotional state of another person, or even that of our self, is severely compromised.

The silver lining of having been a peer-group reject was that I was spared many of the effects of peer pressure, so potent in shaping a person's thinking in adolescence. Being different is a very lonely and difficult experience for a developing individual. Yet it is helpful in distancing someone from the usual benefits of fitting in, as this often comes at the price of forsaking the uniqueness of being your true self. Still, without some sort of affirming and healing experience (such as psychotherapy) which does not rob us of our individuality, the pain of alienation can also lead to a morass of negativity and a sense of being a victim.

On the other hand, if you've been lucky enough to experience 'good enough' parenting, in which you have been held, mirrored, and supported in being yourself from an early age, you can skip this painful experience. I would suggest that in my own case, however, it was the parallel experiences of emotional isolation (and therefore the freedom to think differently from my peer group), and deep-seated emotional distress which set up conditions that challenged me to look for meaning in my life. The interplay of personal, familial, and social forces in a person's early life must be adequately challenging yet also adequately supportive so as not to produce a shutdown of the person's functioning.

Achieving and maintaining one's emotional independence (which does not rule out the interdependence of partnership) is a lifelong project. It requires support from those around us in tandem with recognizing the basic aloneness of the human condition. No matter whether you are a hermit in the desert or living peacefully with your soul mate in an urban area, to be an individual is to be alone with your self. However, this is not the rugged individualism, devil take the hindmost attitude, of Western society. Our being one with all that is *and* being fundamentally alone is one of those paradoxical pairs, requiring a both/and, not an either/or mentality. Understanding and acting from the conviction that whatever we do to someone else, we do to our self (and vice versa), is evidence that we have integrated this paradox.

Fear

Fear is the source of all other painful emotions and, in its most intense form, is the basis of what some call evil. The level of fear which our aloneness generates in us is the single biggest challenge which human beings must come to grips with. This fear, which if not recognized for what it is (an emotion emerging within us), can drive us to a multitude of intellectual, emotional, and behavioural reactions in an effort to get rid of it. The vast majority of these efforts cause more harm than good. I have already outlined a number of these reactions earlier in this book, but let's look at some of the most prominent ones.

At a collective level, patriarchal religions are a good example of a fear-shaped response to an internal sense of fear. They have constructed worldviews, enshrined psychological defence mechanisms, enforced social hierarchies, composed myths, and celebrated rituals which have fostered oppression and environmental destruction the world over for many millennia. But, they have also given people the impression that they can protect themselves from fear, insisting that there is a saviour and identifying the bad guys who are causing your fear. This has made them extremely popular.

Socially, exercising power over other people and the natural world is another negative solution to our fear. This one is best summed up by the phrase 'the best defence is a good offence'. Being in control, dominating others and the environment, and instilling fear in others can give a person the impression that they are in charge of their reality. The accumulation of wealth has become the primary means of exercising power over one's environment, to the point of replacing outright military domination (though this is always a threat in the background). True power, on the other hand, is being able to address our own fear and to take responsibility for the shape of our own life. This allows us to be creative and loving to our self and others and to enhance our environment in a balanced way.

At a personal level, addictions are another significantly destructive solution. The need for altering our mood is fundamentally driven by the discomfort with, and fear of, our fear. The more obvious and commonly identified addictions are the focus of 12-step groups that are filled with people hoping to get a grip on an out of control life. But workaholism, gambling, and the addiction to money have been enshrined as the life blood of our economic system, where the buzz gained by their enactment is hugely rewarded rather than seen as pathological. The central dynamic of addiction is escape. Anything is preferable to actually being with our fear and dealing with it.

Physiologically, fear is hardwired to produce one of three reactions: anger, flight, or collapse. Anger, if it is not expressed, becomes depression. Good children, nice girls, and a host of others, are taught not to be angry. In the Letter to the Ephesians anger is identified as a sin. As an emotion, anger is morally neutral. It's what you do with it that makes the difference. But under the burden of trying to be acceptable socially or morally, many people internalize their anger. This eventually robs them of energy and a zest for life. It can, if allowed to intensify, push a person to suicide.

The solution for fear

Mindfulness is the best tool for learning to simply sit with our fear and observe it. This technique has been pioneered by those who follow the insights of the Buddha. But as we are learning in the West, it is a tool that does not require becoming a Buddhist in order for it to be extremely effective in dealing with fear. Being mindful of fear allows us to disengage with it so that we can *respond* rather than *react*. Our reactions are generally conditioned by our earlier experiences in life.

Our earliest experiences come from childhood when we are physically and emotionally extremely vulnerable and have not yet developed an intellect which is capable of assessing and analysing a situation. These reactions become an autopilot. They are patterns of emotions and behaviours laid down in early childhood which are not primarily responsive to the present situation in later life. Once triggered by even the slightest of similarities with the past they propel us to react without thought or discernment as to their present appropriateness or effectiveness. Often they bring on the very thing that they were originally designed to avoid. For example, a fellow who was made fun of by his dad has developed a habit of doing the same thing to other people to get the jump on them. Do unto others before they do unto you! But then he finds himself being avoided by the people he likes, but can't figure out why.

Jon Kabat-Zinn and Thich Nhat Hanh are probably the two most well-known teachers of mindfulness. They have both produced a considerable number of written and audio titles that will help anyone interested in learning mindfulness to arrive at their goal. The former's approach is more adjusted to the insights of Western psychology whereas the latter's orientation tends to suffer from some of the limitations of Buddhism. One of these is its attitude towards anger which sees it as something to simply be let go of because it is due to wrong perception (see *Anger* by Thich Nhat Hanh, 2001). Unfortunately, since anger is caused by an experience of being under threat, not by simple misperception, this approach cannot work in the long term. Anger is a hardwired response to fear and for those who have been seriously traumatized, anger is a healthy reaction. Not until underlying trauma has been healed can the life-preserving anger be resolved. But a mindful awareness can keep us from lashing out in inappropriate and unhelpful ways after the initial danger is past.

The healing of trauma, which is held in the body until it is resolved, is one of the most pressing health needs of our time. Half of all the people who come to see me for psychotherapy are suffering from serious trauma. It is only recently that we have come to understand the physiology of trauma enough to be able to help a person release it from their body. Without that, the body continues to give a person the feeling that they are in danger from an immediate threat. This source of fear is different from the underlying condition of aloneness.

Intellectual

Intellectually the 1960s and 1970s were extremely stimulating times. Philosophy (especially existentialism which was then the new kid on the philosophical block) was busy challenging all the accepted traditional perspectives. It grappled very consciously with the nature of reality and the meaning of life. This very much suited the kinds of questions I was asking from my aching and depressed wilderness. Now there is constructivism which says it's all packaging so that what you believe doesn't make a difference. At university level questions about the meaning of life and what it means to be a human being are no longer considered to be worthy of investigation. Now, the main point of being educated is to make money, get ahead, and to acquire power and security. Recent statistics show that in the past 30 years there has been a significant increase in undergraduates pursuing degrees in business and engineering, and a decrease in those studying the humanities and social sciences (see F. Donoghue's *The Last Professors*, 2008).

The other wheel to the cart of my intellectual life, of course, was theology. Fortunately, my professors were into the Socratic method – ask questions! And ask questions I did, as scathingly and with as much scepticism as I could muster. But the professors were asking questions too, which made for great discussions. They weren't afraid of questions but saw them as an important tool in gaining deeper insights into reality and the message of Jesus. We explored, and wondered, and marvelled at the complexity of it all.

The only framework which can sustain a person who is questioning everything is a spirituality based on love and experienced in love. It was my very fortunate fate to encounter such a condition. 'God is love' was the only unquestioned assertion in my intellectual universe at that time. It was self-evident, and anything that was attributed to God which contravened this truth was seen to be not true about God, no matter who said it. This included the Bible and Church authorities. Of course, it was the Church authorities who eventually didn't like the kinds of answers that people were beginning to find in their explorations, precisely because they rattled their vested interests.

Down came the axe on any discussion of women's ordination. Anathema was liberation theology, feminist theology, creation theology, or any other theology which didn't uphold the patriarchal authority of presumably celibate old men. But for those of us who had seen the light there was no turning back. The integration of moral theology with developmental psychology provided a whole new framework with which to understand sin and ultimately to replace such a judgemental concept. Stages of moral development were proposed and explored, and then stages of faith development. The paradigm of organic growth resonated with my experience of being rooted in all that is. *External* divine authority was no longer needed. The blueprint is within us.

This is why the regressive move of the Catholic Church under John Paul II was so regrettable and destructive for those seeking a viable spirituality within Christianity. We live at a time when society's and people's understanding of reality are changing at a dizzying pace. If Church leadership had been able to move with the inspiration of love and social justice which can be easily taken from the teachings of Jesus of Nazareth, Roman Catholic Christianity could have become a beacon of hope in an emerging world. Instead it has become one of the religious tools used by the dominant multinationals to oppress people around the globe. Fox News, with its fundamentalist Christian anti-gay and anti-women agenda, spurs on racist/sexist/homophobic bigots who export and fund the same message in Africa, Asia, and Latin America.

The power issues that motivated Popes John Paul II and Benedict XVI are no different from those driving the super wealthy to keep themselves in positions of power and dominance. Today the Roman Catholic Church is barely distinguishable from a host of right-wing Christian fundamentalist sects which control their membership with the fear of hell and condemnation, and promote all manner of bigotry against those who differ from the supposedly godly individual. It remains to be seen whether or not Francis I will really be able to break with this legacy. Functionally faithful Roman Catholics and avowed Christians are often very rigid and emotionally insecure, guided only by the words of their saviour's mouthpiece.

Of course the style of leadership required in an environment of seeking and pondering is very different from the type favoured and used by those who see themselves as the voice on earth of an absolute God. Leadership in a world discovering its own divinity needs men and women grounded not only in the wisdom of the past, but also in their own shared divinity. Leaders need to support people's sense of dignity and validity as well as challenging behaviour which oppresses others or the planet. A knowledge of history and the mistakes made therein are excellent guideposts for balancing self-confidence with humility.

The loss of an intellectual system based on love and championing social justice leaves a gaping hole in the range of options open to young people who are currently searching for answers to their questions about the meaning of life. Today those teaching theology in a Roman Catholic university must take an oath of fidelity to the Church. No rocking of the boat is allowed.

In terms of an intellectual frame of reference, Buddhism illustrates that one does not need an absolutist approach in order to have a workable spirituality. There is no deity in Buddhism, though sometimes the Buddha can take on this role for those who emotionally need a sense of infallibility in their guide. Some have described Buddhism as more a philosophy and a psychology than a religion because it does not involve a deity. However, since my operating definition of spirituality is 'a story by which we make sense of living and dying', then Buddhism obviously qualifies. It has already contributed much to the health of contemporary spirituality, but like the others has gaps which need to be addressed.

Spiritual

My understanding of things spiritual and my participation in spiritual practices were shaped by Vatican II and its rapid shake-up of emphasis and understanding within Roman Catholic spiritual practices. There was a pronounced effort on the part of the Council to return to the basics of the Christian message: the primacy of the individual's relationship to God, Jesus' concern for the poor, and the local Church community as the container of the presence of Christ. The Mass was repackaged as the Eucharist, the community's celebration of the presence of their Christ among them. This was an attempt to see the Mass as a fellowship celebration like the Last Supper in Christian Scripture rather than as a sacrifice to appease an angry god. The use of the local language, the facing of the priest to the people, and the kiss of peace exchanged by those present, highlighted the importance of community. The Mass, rather than a host of novenas and festivals, was the way the community was to worship.

The importance of social justice was also brought into sharp focus. This reminded people that religious practice could not make up for the oppression of their neighbour. Latin America had the inspiration of its liberation theology, with the basic Christian community restructuring the Church away from being a clergy-led entity to being the assembly of the people. Hierarchy was a foreign structure in this context. This breathed new life and vitality into the Church, which in turn began to challenge social injustice. Again, the Church hierarchy felt threatened by their loss of status in this approach and decided that the only social issue relevant for Catholics was that of abortion (and much later, homosexuality). Now, even if the woman (or girl) has been made pregnant by rape or incest, Catholic 'social justice' is only concerned with the following of its own narrowly defined rules.

The shift in prayer practices was, however, perhaps the most important change. Rather than reciting pre-packaged words, begging for forgiveness or favours, prayer came to be seen as the dialogue in one's heart with Christ and/or God. The use of intermediaries, saints, and angels of all stripes, was considered unnecessary and inferior to a more heart-to-heart conversation. God's loving aspect was brought to the fore and the angry, judging God was downplayed. This had huge import for an individual who embarked on a spiritual life. As I began to sit with my sense of Jesus and God I was taken into myself by exploring the generosity of divine love.

I also had a few mystical experiences of my own where the sense of the presence of Jesus or God was extremely powerful. My sense of connectedness with God grew and deepened as I spent more time in conversation. This was probably what most directly led to my experience of being 'God as Jesus was God'. When I mentioned my separation from the Church my father was worried about how I would stay in touch with 'God's grace'. For those who have been assured that the Church (read 'priest') is a necessary intermediary for this, 'no salvation outside the walls' (see *Catechism of the Catholic Church*) is what keeps them in line. But for anyone who has seen their own divinity, the priests lose their power.

Fortunately, I still had my sense of loving and being loved which helped orient me in these new waters. My sense was that I needed to continue improving my ability to love others and to love myself. Perhaps this is a good place to say more specifically what I mean by this much bandied about word. Love, for me, is composed of a sense of liking, compassion, and empathy. Generally, even the most difficult person has likeable aspects which can be focused on as long as it does not make us blind to any underlying threat they might pose. But even while we are maintaining our boundaries or holding another responsible for their actions, we can have a sense of their being a fellow human being to whom we are connected. It is an awareness of our connectedness to one another at a very deep level which is the most fundamental meaning of love.

Empathy is when we can emotionally tune into this connectedness. But even when we can't, a conscious acknowledgement of our common humanity prevents us from doing to others what we would not want done to our self. This would vastly reduce adversarial violence and make communication, conversation, and mediation the preferred alternative.

Compassion is very similar to empathy but is a more collective experience. We can have empathy for someone with whom we are conversing or looking at and this can move us to action on their behalf. But compassion allows us to resonate with those whom we have never met but whose distress we have known in ourselves. The taking of action in response to our sense of compassion is tempered by our own learning process in which we have discovered the wisdom of personal experience. Sometimes it is helpful to allow another person to understand a situation for themselves by working their own way through it, as long as this will not result in serious or irreversible damage to the other or our own financial gain.

Stages of faith

In addition to stages of emotional development and moral development, a fellow by the name of James Fowler published his research into possible stages of faith development in 1981. His long-term project tried to discern whether or not there is a process of development in the type of belief system that appeals to people as they mature psychologically and spiritually. He identified the following stages.

First stage: Intuitive-Projective faith

Fowler was unable to study children under two years old as part of the project because, due to their limited vocabulary, they were unable to converse properly. So he called this a 'pre-stage' and used developmental psychology and attachment theory instead. These disciplines view this time in a child's life as the starting point for a person's ability to trust, hope, relate to other beings, and know what it is like to participate in love. Fowler saw the first stage of faith development starting from the age of two. It is one in which the child recognizes and interacts with emotionally charged pictures and symbols. A child can recognize a picture of a parent but there is also the reaction to scary faces and loud sounds. The child is beginning to deal with the forces of fear and security. Often powerful experiences from ages two to seven stay with us for the rest of our lives and leave a visual imprint for what is good and what is terrifying. It is a time of 'just so' stories and so is called the Intuitive-Projective stage of faith.

Second stage: Mythic-Literal faith

At around the age of seven children's brains gradually become physically capable of rational thought, and they start to figure out when something is true or is a product of their imagination, or when someone is trying to fool them. Thus they transition to what is known as operational thinking. Concretely, this means they can now understand the logical construct of 'if x then y'. If you touch a hot surface, then you will get burned. They are also able to understand and appreciate simple stories. Most importantly, they can tell the story of their own experience. Generally the terms of their stories are primarily drawn from the stories they hear in their living situation. What they hear Mother or Dad saying about themselves or other people is taken in uncritically, and there is no other possible way to understand the situation. They are incapable of reflecting on what is being said, and putting it into a historical or social context. Reality is black and white. There are goodies and baddies, and you don't want to be the baddie! Baddies get punished. This is considered to be the second stage of how human beings believe the world works, and which Fowler called 'Mythic-Literal faith'.

Stage three: Synthetic-Conventional faith

This stage becomes an option around the time of puberty, when the physically developing brain takes another leap into the ability to think abstractly, that is, the ability to imagine contrary-to-fact possibilities. As adolescents begin to come into contact with stories other than their own, it can occur to them that what they think may not be the only way to understand how reality functions. A teenager from a devout family may hear an atheist speak. In addition, crafting their own story is an important part of their identity formation as they come to grips with making their way in the world. If they are overly dependent on their peer group or their family or any other authority figure, they may fall into a very rigid approach to whatever story they sign up to at this time. Because of this Fowler called stage three the Synthetic-Conventional faith.

Stage four: Individuated-Reflective faith

Hopefully, when a person leaves home or finds that the institution that champions their faith story isn't as infallible or righteous as it says it is, they will begin to become self-reflective. They will see that they need to take responsibility for what they believe, and not simply go along with the group for the sake of belonging. This is a crucial pivot point in one's emotional and spiritual development and one that many never arrive at. It requires a certain level of emotional security that is based on one's own individuality rather than on one's connection to a group, partner, or family. The question on the mat is: is there an absolute truth, or do we have to work with uncertainty? This requires a demythologizing of stories that previously were taken as literally true. A person works with the spirit of the story rather than simply with its literal understanding. And so this fourth stage is called Individuated-Reflective faith.

Stage five: Conjunctive faith

Even with this level of sophistication, life, if allowed, will continue to challenge our well-ordered ideas and carefully constructed boxes. Life is messy. All sorts of contradictions will come into focus; paradoxes will taunt us at inconvenient times. Deaths occur, bad luck, ill health, haunting dreams … As we get to know ourselves through the years we notice that we make the same mistakes over and over. In this way, we become aware of unconscious forces at work in us. The ability to understand that there are parts of ourselves that we aren't familiar with, but which often heavily influence our choices, or show up in projections onto other people, is evidence that we are becoming emotionally and psychologically mature. We no longer see the world as black and white, right and wrong, true and not true. At this point, we can tolerate the fact that things aren't the way we thought they were. We can see relative merits and restrictions to everything out there and to ourselves. This stage is one of Conjunctive faith, which allows us to respond to reality as we meet it rather than imposing our shoulds and oughts on it.

Stage six: Mystical Union faith

Fowler's last stage of faith was one he found so few examples of in terms of the people he actually spoke to, that he included it mostly due to examples from history. In this stage, the person has a sense of being one with the divine so he called it Mystical Union. For those who don't think in terms of a deity there are phrases like 'one with all that is'. Since the last phrase doesn't provoke the same sense of scepticism as saying that one is united to 'god', it is perhaps easier for people to sense that this is their experience. Quantum physics tells us that everything in the universe is interconnected. Two electrons that split from one another nevertheless continue to affect one another despite being light years apart. Whatever you do to whomever or whatever is around you, you do to yourself.

Methods

There can be no doubt that how we live our life, what we do with our time and energy, the goals we set for our self, and the sort of person we wish to become, will play a major role in the outcome of our life. No matter what disasters or boons come our way, it is how we respond to life, based on our vision for the kind of person we wish to be, that will be the ultimate determiner of our life's journey. The other major contributor to the shape of our psyche will be the people with whom we choose to associate in relationships of greater or lesser intimacy.

The volume of writing addressing what a true believer needs to do and how to act to gain salvation/enlightenment or reduce karma and escape the cycle of birth and death, etc. is truly huge. There are often guidelines in the form of spiritual practices which indicate how a person can make progress in the spiritual life. I will look at some of the basic principles found in such guidelines and reflect on their suitability in an evolving spirituality. However, the most powerful forces shaping people's ideals in life today come from advertising, rather than any religion.

For those coming from a traditional Catholic Christian approach, there has been a great emphasis on suffering and the mortification of the flesh in order to atone for their sins. This is said to allow one to be purified for entrance into heaven, generally only available after death. In this valley of tears, suffering is the highest path to heaven. Another suggestion is that one would engage in the corporal and spiritual works of mercy in order to convey the love of God for all creatures, an *imitatio Christi*, the imitation of Christ, 'by whose [sacrificial] blood you have been saved' (Romans 5). The main drawbacks with these approaches are the devaluing of the body, the impoverishment of one's self-esteem, and the disempowerment of the individual in a hierarchy of more powerful beings (both human and divine).

Other spiritual paths, such as the Jewish and Hindu, focus more on the keeping of laws and ritual practices. The great debates on the minutia of the Torah down through the centuries are mind-numbing stuff. And the disengagement of worship from personal integrity and social justice issues leaves no connection between religion and behaviour in the rest of life. This compartmentalized approach does not integrate religion or spirituality into the fabric of a maturing individual; such an approach is not healthy for the person or the collective. It is more reminiscent of obsessive-compulsive disorder (OCD), in which a person worries and repeats actions over and over again in an effort to reassure themselves that they are, or will be, safe.

Once again, Buddhism has a lot to recommend it in terms of insights into psychology and the energy systems of the body as well as in mindfulness meditation. But it also has some serious drawbacks. The biggest of these is the pursuit of the 'no-self'. In the West, this is interpreted as abandoning the ego. But you cannot lose yourself until you find yourself. Despite the rugged individualism promoted in the US, most people there still operate from a persona, or superficial self, that is primarily shaped by consumerism and the needs of a wounded inner child. The worst thing a person at this stage of development can do is forsake their underdeveloped ego. Another drawback is its approach to anger. (For this discussion see pages 39 and 108–9.)

Christianity, among other religions, has urged people to view the ego and/or the body negatively, seeing it as the source of rebellion, the tool of the devil, or at the very least, the fly in the ointment. But in fact, when you begin to address the healing process of emotionally wounded humans (which are all of us) the most important task to be achieved is that of growing a healthily functioning ego. What is criticized as selfishness or self-centredness is actually narcissism or an underdeveloped ego which is desperately trying to fill the gaping hole of its unmet emotional needs. This is where the ability to truly love one's self is crucial in coming to wholeness or holiness, grounded in one's entire being, rather than from the dictates of a thinking-based, life-denying religion. It is only after a person has found her or his individual self that they can then go on to transcend it in a healthy way.

This, of course, also rules out all communities which insist that a person submit to the resident guru in order to attain enlightenment or hand over all their money in order to have access to the secrets of healing, power, or immortality. Community life can be a very powerful tool for self-development *if* it respects the individual's autonomy and dignity. Learning when to compromise and when to stand one's ground is part of the journey to self-awareness. There is also the benefit of being with other people who want to use the same approach to living as you do. Learning from those who have been at this for a longer time can be extremely useful. But at the end of the day we must also be attentive to the inner voice that protests when we have compromised something vital within ourselves.

Many New Age approaches make use of energy work, interaction with spirit guides, past life information, or aids like flower essences. These can be quite helpful and effective in helping to decrease our fear or the physical effects of it on our bodies. Affirmations and guided imagery, or visualizations, are used to train our underlying beliefs and expectations of life into positive and life enhancing realities. The power of positive thinking can be easily demonstrated as key to creating a reality for ourselves which is growth-filled and deepening. But these cannot in and of themselves heal the emotional wounds and deficits of childhood. Inner child work, in some form, is required (see J. Bradshaw's *Homecoming*, 1991).

Working with a good psychotherapist is probably the most effective way to make progress on our healing journey. It is one of the best ways to discover the defence mechanisms which we use, and to uncover the ways in which our fear controls our life and our perceptions. I have found that stretches of such work, interspersed with time to integrate it in simply living day to day, have provided a good balance of introspection and a full-on engagement with the nuts and bolts of living.

On a number of occasions I have recommended psychotherapy as a very helpful tool for self-healing and personal growth. As I indicated earlier, the numerous differences in approaches within psychotherapy leave a person in nearly the same quandary as trying to choose a spirituality. From my long years participating in psychotherapy, both as client and therapist, the following is a summary of my recommendations. It has been my observation that Freudian-based psychoanalysis is not effective. I have found Jungian analysis to be effective but I have also discovered that the same effectiveness can be achieved in a much shorter time. For emotional healing, I have found that three levels need to be addressed.

The first step in a healing journey is to stop all addictive behaviours. Substances such as drugs and alcohol are the most obvious but other compulsive behaviours also need to be challenged. In tandem with giving up unhealthy coping skills, developing a healthy one is crucial. Mindfulness is the most effective coping skill as more and more research is starting to demonstrate. The ability to change requires disconnecting from our autopilots so that we can choose a different way to deal with the present moment.

Next, any trauma in the body must be dealt with. Unless the physiological basis of that type of fear is healed, there will be very little or no progress in coming to grips with our sense of aloneness in the world. An obvious corollary is that if someone is living in an unsafe environment, with, for example, ongoing domestic violence or abuse of any kind, or grinding poverty or environmental poisons, significant healing is extremely unlikely.

Finally, learning to love ourselves is the most basic form of emotional healing. Inner child work is the most time-sensitive way to do this. Since it generally requires the help of a psychotherapist to be effective, economic considerations need to be taken into account. However, without competent outside guidance what tends to happen in inner child work is a repeat of how we were parented the first time around, which, if it had been good enough, would preclude the need to do inner child work in the first place.

Even with holistic approaches in psychology and cosmology there is no substitute for the practice of meditation, either mindfulness or something similar, in the cultivation of the spiritual life. Only by sitting with one's self and the struggle of attempting stillness and self-awareness can all the intellectual and psychological progress be integrated. We are very fortunate to have the experience of Jill Bolte Taylor, a neuroanatomist, (see her TED talk and book) who had the misfortune in 1996 to suffer a stroke. It was in the left hemisphere of her brain, affecting her language centre. As the stroke shut down that side of her brain, she found herself experiencing an entirely present moment sensation of being connected to the universe which was very blissful. When the left hemisphere managed to regain some functioning, she was once again looking at life through her rational mind, based in an ego perspective on reality. These two perspectives alternated for her a number of times, and helped her to understand that the left brain grounds our experience of being an individual while the right brain is where we connect with a more mystical, holistic being in the universe.

When we are able to quieten the concerns of our rational mind, we can access an entirely different way of being in the world. This option is grounded in our biology.

This is a very exciting breakthrough in our understanding of our possibilities for relating to reality. It is just as valid as the rational side of our brain. The benefits of entering this alternate reality are numerous. It gives us access to a stress-free zone that allows our bodies a respite from the sort of tension that constantly harms our immune system and continually increases our distress. It also allows us to be aware that we are connected to all that is, as well as tapping into a well of compassion and bliss. This can help us keep our batteries charged for the challenges of living in the modern world.

Generally speaking, however, I would have no recommendation in terms of rituals or spiritual paths. As long as what you do is guided by love and compassion for yourself, others, and the environment, the ways in which this can be ritualized are unlimited. This brings to mind St Augustine's advice in the fifth century to 'love and do what you will'. Unfortunately, this was his way of justifying war, which I obviously would not agree with. Love has to be more than a value to which one intellectually ascribes. There can be no justification for war as the usual causes are factors which have not been addressed responsibly.

Arrival point

When someone has achieved success or acceptance into the ranks of those who have excelled at something, people will say that 'they have arrived!' Many religions make use of terms which indicate that a person has arrived at the highest level of spiritual development. Christianity talks about a 'unitive stage of the mystical life' to indicate that a person is very close to God. After their death, they may even be made a saint. Eastern traditions use words that translate as 'enlightenment', to be in a state of 'nirvana'. In New Age parlance, the appellations are 'highly evolved being', 'ascended master', or 'guru' (borrowed from the Sanskrit). But I would question the wisdom of making a fuss about who is a more highly evolved being than others.

We are all travellers on the road and I would hold that the road extends well beyond earth-based lifetimes. While we may find someone helpful on our journey, putting someone on a pedestal is extremely unhelpful for both them and us. Very few people, even those of great integrity, can withstand the unbalancing experience of receiving adulation and exaltation. On the other hand, considering someone else as superior to you shows a profound misunderstanding of who you are. Treating all fellow travellers with respect is the most basic indication of emotional health and integrity. This does not mean that we allow ourselves to be manipulated by aggressive, greedy, or domineering people who have not discovered that what they do to others, they do to themselves. Simple assertiveness is required of us in order to maintain our self-love which does not allow us to become victims.

The best indicator of enlightenment would seem to be a sense of contentment with one's self in the present moment. This doesn't mean that we aren't visited by bouts of fear based on our vulnerability in being a separate individual. But even with that, our response is one of mindfulness, and patient being with, rather than depression, escape, or projection onto a scapegoat. A sense of compassion would be another essential component of having come into our self. This then takes us on to supporting social justice and ecologically sustainable lifestyles. These can be attained without spending mountains of money or travelling to far places. But certainly some separation from the familiar is often useful, and some prioritizing of our time, effort, and money is required. Self-development and spiritual maturity are not a consumerist activity. If you are committed to healing and growth it will come your way – seek and you will find, ask and you will receive, knock and it will be opened to you.

For the first two years of my time in Boston there was an unrelenting ache in my heart. I had dreams in which I was trying to explain to my religious sisters why I had to leave. It was a difficult time, but Nina, my Jungian analyst, helped me to weather this transition and use such brokenness as an entry into greater self-knowledge and ever deeper healing. And it worked! On looking back at these first five-plus years in Boston, I observed from the comfort of my own apartment:

> *February 15 1993*
>
> Journeying still. [After rereading my earlier reflections, I am] Embarrassed by my ardour, touched by my pain, moved by my poetry. It does seem that all those things-have-been-healed-in-me passages finally seem to have accumulated to something. Analysis really was a turning point. I seem to have grown up somewhat and find myself a therapist. Kundalini winds closer to me inside and out. My frame of reference for reality has changed so drastically that old friends react with dismay. This is hard to cope with when the new frame of reference still pricks me with its weirdness. They tell me I am a woman of power, and a healer. I am afraid to believe that.

> So many years of wandering, so many times of wounding and dying. Yet through it all the red thread of my intense dedication to the All, to the Love which plays our realities in and out of sight. Through it all, I have endeavoured more than anything else to be true to the One who calls. So be it.

The New Age isn't a coherent set of beliefs that one ascribes to. The New Age as I encountered it in Boston through the 1990s was a very varied phenomenon with hundreds of people putting out their own experiences and constructs for public consumption. Most of these share certain basic assumptions – multiple lifetimes, energy levels beyond the physical, and communication with beings on a spiritual plane. The vast majority of these are in aid of healing our human woundedness. Picking up on the newly developed approaches to psychological healing in the first half of the twentieth century, they had expanded well beyond to include spiritually oriented approaches to life, liberty, and the pursuit of happiness.

There were so many people in the Boston area interested in exploring this new collection of ideas and practices that there was an adult education centre solely dedicated to New Age information and techniques. This provided me with an excellent opportunity to deepen and broaden my investigation of what was on offer. As I moved through a number of courses, read numerous books, and began to form friendships with the people I met on the courses, I was able to gradually piece together specific tools that I found helpful. Foremost among these was the nature-based approach of Machaelle Small Wright and her centre, Perelandra, in Virginia. Her personal story is interesting and unconventional. But I have made use of her approach for many years and it seems to have enhanced my healing journey significantly. If it works I use it. (If I use tentative language with regard to any approach, it is because I am generally using more than one approach at any given time, so it's hard to know where the effectiveness comes from. Quite possibly it is 'all of the above'.) Certainly her understanding of nature meshes well with that found among aboriginal peoples as well as more contemporary thinkers such as Rupert Sheldrake and his 'morphic resonances'. Her system also provides me with a bit of ritual celebration, focused on the times of the equinoxes and solstices.

During my early years in Boston, I also engaged in some genealogical research. My father's father had been born in a town north of Boston. My brother Joe had provided me with our great-grandfather's name, so I began with the 1900 census. His entry came up on the index as 'Danvers Insane Hospital' – not what I was expecting, but then not entirely a surprise as I thought more about it. From this less than auspicious start, I gradually progressed to learning a lot about this branch of my family. My great-grandmother, Frances Levinia Berry, had come from Moncton, New Brunswick, probably on the train built especially to transport Maritime Canadians to the mills of New England. She'd had a hard life, and was buried in an unmarked grave. I organized her grandchildren and we put a gravestone on it. I also wrote up her story, in a sympathetic voice. It felt like one of the pieces of energy that had brought me to Boston had been honoured.

So it seemed that I would settle down in Boston, having connected with family in the form of my father's half-cousin and his wife (whose parents were from Ireland). But then the dreams started.

Chapter 9

Interacting with Other People: Social Justice

If you want peace, work for justice.

Henry Louis Mencken

I would suggest that social justice is the most important contribution which the Judeo-Christian tradition has made to Western religion and spirituality. While there is some interest in social justice in other traditions, only in this one is it said to be the highest form of worship, and the summation of the entire Law of the Jews:

> *So in everything, do to others what you would have them do to you, for this sums up the Law and the Prophets.*
>
> (*NIV*, Matthew 7:12)

Just to make clearer the revolutionary nature of what Jesus is quoted as saying here, let's look at what the Law and the Prophets meant in the time of Jesus. The Law, or the Torah, is the first five books of the Hebrew Testament, that is, Genesis, Exodus, Leviticus, Numbers, and Deuteronomy. Although they are presented as describing the early events in the history of the Jewish people, they were written long after the purported events.

For example, Abraham has generally been dated to around 1800 BCE, and Moses to around 1200 BCE, yet it is now thought that the books were written sometime after the eighth century BCE. More recently it has been discovered that there is no archaeological evidence for either Abraham or Moses, very little for David, and none for Solomon. It has been demonstrated that stable groups can pass on accurate information for 10,000 years (Reid, 'Ancient Aboriginal stories preserve history of a rise in sea level', in C. Moseley, ed. *OGMIOS Newsletter* 58, Dec. 2015). But it is difficult to know if the Hebrew tribes were a stable enough society to accurately remember the stories of their ancestors, especially due to the political instability of that geographic area in those centuries. Yet it is possible that this information could have been kept in memory by oral tradition whereby the group's ancestral happenings were told and retold by those charged with committing them to memory. Such prodigious feats of memory were commonplace before the invention of writing or printing. However, a number of the details in the text, including historical ones, often reflect conditions at the time in which they were actually written down. This is why all sorts of anachronistic details have crept into the text.

In addition to setting the stage of Jewish religious history, the Torah also includes all the rules about religious sacrifice as well as the rules about what is ritually 'clean' and 'unclean'. Everything else written about how Jews should worship, and what they believe, is based on these five books.

In the Hebrew Testament the Prophets contain the recounting of the activities of men who were said to speak the word of the Lord. Samuel was the first prophet and his most significant activity was guiding the Israelites through the transition from being a collection of tribes, led by 'judges', or wise warriors of individual tribes, to having a king. He anointed the first king, Saul, but then deposed him on advice from Yahweh and anointed David instead.

Thus, the first recorded Hebrew prophet was a diviner of Yahweh's will, which included being a 'king maker'. However, in terms of their actual presentation, the early prophets bore more resemblance to those 'possessed by the spirit' among present day tribal peoples than to your local psychic, or a card-reading fortune teller. These men did not write down their prophecies, as they were most probably illiterate. They would have started out in the vein of those spirit-possessed individuals who generally tend to the wild side.

However, as Israel, along with Judah after the civil war and resulting split, became a more settled people, their wealth increased.

As Samuel (in his more negative response to the institution of the monarchy) had warned, the kings lorded it over the people. They imposed taxes, and construction projects were undertaken, building things like the temple and a palace. As in every other urban society, some people became richer than others, and economic inequality became more pronounced.

In addition, as part of diplomatic exchanges, the king took on foreign wives who brought their goddess with them. So the earlier prophets said that the country would suffer defeat because of a lack of faithfulness to Yahweh and to heartfelt religious observance. But later prophets began to severely criticize an affluent Israel for their treatment of the poor and downtrodden. There are thus two parallel approaches to the meaning of true religion in the prophets recorded in the Hebrew Bible. One emphasizes what is usually thought of as religious observance: ritual, sacrifice, offerings, the saying of prayers. The other equates the word of Yahweh with social justice. How the wealthy treat the poor is more important than religious observance. From a purely historical point of view, of course, due to the political dynamics of the Middle East at that time, Israel and Judah would have been taken over by the local empires, no matter what course of behaviour they might have followed.

It is the difference of focus found in these two approaches which has been the primary tension among the followers of Jesus. One could arguably say that Jesus himself came down firmly on the side of social justice as the meaning of true religion, whereas the early Christian Church seized upon what they saw as his sacrificial death as being the most important reason for his existence. This is where many people make the distinction between what Jesus was about and what Christianity is about. The compromise sometimes taken by Christianity is what has been called the 'corporal works of mercy'. In this approach, the wealthy are expected to give some of their excess to the poor and support charitable institutions but there is no challenge to their domination of the society.

Someone like Mother Teresa would be a good example of this. She often wheedled large sums of money from the wealthy to support her work among the poor. This made them feel good in that they were being generous to the less fortunate. But she never criticized the rigged rules of society which allowed the wealthy their gross excess, or to get away with murder, often implicit in the exploitation of their workers. Whereas those who look at a bigger, systemic picture said that society should be changed to make it a more level playing field. The very fact of huge economic inequality is identified as the key issue. Liberation theology, which evolved in Latin America, saw the social justice focus of Jesus as being the true 'good news' that he had come to preach.

When I went looking for the source of the social justice theme in the Jewish prophets, for a long time I could find nothing relevant to my question. It was not until I came across *Religion in Human Evolution*, by Robert Bellah (2011) that some light was forthcoming on this topic. Bellah was a well-known and respected sociologist of religion, and in this, his magnum opus, he has looked at how religious expression has evolved in and with the growth of human society, starting from very early Palaeolithic times (i.e., from roughly 2.5 million to 10,000 years ago). It is a serious, scholarly work yet also well attuned to the lived reality of the development of religion.

Bellah documented that the concern for social justice is something inherent in human society, manifesting whenever there has been an imbalance in either power or wealth among the members of a community. In hunter-gatherer groups, this led to the powerful individuals enforcing an egalitarian balance on each other, so that no one person would dominate. None of them wanted to be dominated so therefore they did not allow anyone to be dominant. It was only when the Agrarian Revolution (starting 12,000 years ago) led to a significant increase in the population of communities that the face-to-face nature of relationships diminished. This allowed one powerful man to enlist the support of a minority in a community so that he could dominate the rest of the group. He could then reward his supporters with the substantial surplus that farming had made possible in the society.

Bellah speaks of the 'disposition to dominate' as well as the 'disposition to nurture'. The urge to dominate evidently is inherent in some human beings, perhaps the side effect of testosterone. However, even the urge to nurture requires some dominating, for example when teaching offspring limits, or enforcing safety for as yet inexperienced children. In adulthood, assertiveness requires some use of dominance type energy in order to keep from being dominated by others. What is required is a balance so that individuals are neither too aggressive nor too passive.

From the very earliest times of archaic kingship (the earliest examples in the West that we know of are 5,000 years ago in Sumer and then Egypt), the concern for fairness and social balance within a society were seen as grounded in the religious nature of human society. The king himself was meant to nurture his society, just as the gods were expected to be concerned for the welfare of their people. But as societies grew and developed, imbalances inevitably crept in. It was primarily the marginal members of a society who then raised the issue of justice within the society. Their marginality could have been the result of their lifelong circumstances or it could have been personally chosen.

In the case of the major prophets of Israel it was experienced as a calling from their god. Thus Jesus was continuing in this line of his religious tradition which specifically linked social justice with the essence of their religion. This is then seen as an inherent part of ethical monotheism. In Athenian democracy social balance was not seen as something of primary concern to the Greek gods so it was not connected to their religion.

Moral development

In the late twentieth century, Lawrence Kohlberg, a professor at Harvard University, engaged in research to discover whether or not there were stages of development in moral reasoning and resulting behaviour. His theory of moral development has been succinctly laid out by R. Barger, a professor at the University of Notre Dame, and describes six stages, which are grouped into three levels of moral awareness.

Level one

Young children, before the age of six or seven, simply react to their environment in a way that best meets their emotional and physical needs and cannot be said to be moral in the true sense of the word. The age of reason sees the appearance of the first level of moral development in which children respond to the dictates of authority figures, and they comply out of fear of punishment or of the disapproval of, or loss of attention from, a valued adult. In the second stage of this level, right behaviour is seen as being in one's best interest. Those who obey the rules get rewarded.

Level two

In the second level of moral functioning, people do what others expect them to do, to avoid social stigma, to maintain group membership, or because they see it as their duty. Then, in a second stage of the second level, people consider that laws and rules ought to be obeyed simply because they have been enacted. This is what Kohlberg called the 'conventional' level of moral behaviour and it is the level of development from which the majority of people in Western society have operated. With the 'Reagan Revolution' in the US, greed became good within the upper echelons of government and business. This means that convention was reversed among those groups so that what had previously been seen as wrong was then seen as acceptable, even recommended. Those who obeyed the rules of the time, for example being honest, paying taxes, enacting laws for the common good rather than just for the wealthy, gradually lost power in the society, both politically and financially.

Level three

Kohlberg's reflection was that many people never get to the third level of moral development which involves an understanding of social mutuality and a genuine interest in the welfare of others. Yet as we can see, social mutuality is what the golden rule 'do unto others' is all about. So despite the large number of people who consider themselves Christians, they in fact generally have not reached the level of moral development that Jesus has enjoined on them. They follow rules, claimed to be the will of God based on the Bible, which oppress certain segments of society, especially people of colour and women, with no allowance for birth control or abortion, or people of alternative sexual orientation. Even in the Christian Scripture Jesus is seen to cause scandal because he associated with prostitutes and tax collectors. He wasn't preaching salvation through his death to them because it hadn't yet happened. Instead he was walking his talk: social acceptance and tolerance for those judged as unacceptable by the religious and political leaders of his time. But if a person hasn't developed to this level of moral awareness, they just don't get it.

Interestingly, there has been a good deal of research on the difference in moral reasoning between progressives and conservatives in the US. Conservatives are seen to be very authority oriented, which would put them at the most basic stage of moral development that Kohlberg has described, typical of school-age children. Bob Altemeyer, a university professor, asked people (who self-selected as being of one or the other of these two groups) questions about how they felt about various political and social phenomena. He published the results of his research in his work, *The Authoritarians* (2006), which draws the psychological profiles of those who identify as social, religious or right-wing conservatives. He thereby documented how people who function at that level of moral development are much more influenced by their emotional reactions to events or facts than those who can dispassionately consider information as they receive it.

Since Altemeyer published his study in 2006 there have been many more studies that look at the differences between these two groups, coming at it from a number of different angles, including brain physiology. This research consistently finds that people who are very conservative are much more fear-based in their view of the world and have little tolerance for ambiguity and diversity. This is even reflected in the physiology of their brain development.

Kohlberg's highest stage of moral development is one in which a person is guided by 'respect for universal principles of justice and the demands of individual conscience'. Kohlberg found very few people who operated from this point of view. It requires a high level of emotional development and individuation in a person. It means doing the right thing even when others don't support you or you lose out economically or socially. The universal principle of respect for each person's life and dignity must be held over religious principles that privilege some people over others, for example men over women, whites over people of colour or heterosexuals over homosexuals. The issue of abortion is thornier, as reflected in public opinion in the US. But the production of too many children is a major factor in our ecological crisis. And forcing a woman to have a child which she doesn't want, for whatever reason, is guaranteed to enforce a very distressed life on that child. If a child is not wanted they will pay the psychological price of this wound, which often then becomes a problem for the larger society.

What is social justice?

I would suggest that social justice comes down to two basic issues: in-group/out-group dynamics (or 'us and them') and money/power. Some biological basis has been found for responding fairly and compassionately to people to whom we are related or who are 'people like us', our in-group. But unfortunately the built-in instinct when it comes to everyone else is one of hostility. This means that we have to be able to overcome a certain built-in prejudice against those who are different from us. It is a tribally based instinct that has outlived its usefulness, as seen from a more morally developed point of view.

That statement assumes that there is a moral high ground in human functioning. While this may be intellectually agreed to in some cases, in groups where there is a high level of fear, it will not be the done thing, no matter what Jesus has to say! The parable of the Good Samaritan comes to mind. There is very little real reason for fear in the world today as there is actually enough food to go around if there were the political will to make it happen. Life expectancy has also been greatly extended, though the actual event of death still scares most people. In fact, most of the fear in the world today is artificially induced and fostered. And it is done for one reason and for one reason only – the making of more and more money for the very wealthy. Religious motivations for war have been there for a long time, but the actual waging of war can't happen without arms merchants and others who make a lot of money from it, along with their political servants.

Social injustice has been endemic in the world for millennia and was recently addressed in Western societies with the rise of democracies. The notion that some people were inherently more worthy of respect or power was firmly rejected. The early twentieth century saw the rise of labour protests and unionization which launched a century of improved living conditions for many in Europe and North America. However, when capitalists could no longer oppress people in these areas they increased their bullyboy tactics in the developing world. This has resulted in the growth of Islamic fundamentalism and other efforts to resist exploitation by foreign-based firms. Any resistance to corporate exploitation is now labelled 'terrorism' so that the military/industrial complex can continue to make money from the situation. Nevertheless, the success of business in the 'Third World' was such that slowly business owners exported almost all jobs to those countries, leaving a gradually deteriorating standard of living in Europe and North America.

While resistance to worker exploitation is becoming more organized across the globe, in the US there is still a significant portion of the population which supports the wealthy in the exploitation of themselves. This is done by using the media to convince a percentage of white Americans that people of colour are the cause of their deteriorating economic conditions. In fact, it is the financial elite who have caused the white middle class's demise through their exporting of jobs and tax avoidance practices.

This has created a disparity between the bottom 40 per cent of Americans and the top one per cent that is now quite breath-taking, and much higher than most people are aware. In 2011, the top 20 per cent owned 80 per cent of the wealth in the US. Further, the rate at which this disparity is increasing has grown (Elizabeth Gudrais in *Harvard Magazine*, 2011). In 2014, the Institute for Policy Studies reported that the top 0.1 per cent take home more than 184 times that of the bottom 90 per cent of the US population (at inequality.org). In January 2016, Oxfam reported that just the 62 wealthiest people in the world own more than the 3.5 billion people in the bottom half of the world's income scale. (P. Cohen in *New York Times*, 2016).

Racism is a very handy tool for pitting the middle class against people of colour. The easily manipulated in-group instinct of those feeling the squeeze of a constantly deteriorating standard of living makes people of colour credible targets. Bigotry is further bolstered by Christian fundamentalism which lends apparent righteousness to the cause. As noted previously, the Judeo-Christian approach has a long history of scapegoating and violence against out-groups.

Debt

Debt has been the main way in which those with material resources, or money, have gained power over other people. When the 'have-nots' are lured to products either by their own desires, by psychologically manipulative advertising, or by basic survival needs, they end up borrowing from the 'haves' in order to acquire those goods. Money was introduced to quantify this debt. There is a really excellent history of debt by David Graeber, *Debt: The First 5,000 Years* (2011). In this thorough investigation he has finally brought much needed light to one of the most central social and economic problems of all human society and not just Western society. He first shows how debt language has invaded almost every level of human interaction, including the religious ('forgive us our debts, as we forgive our debtors'). The basic image to explain salvation in Christianity is likewise based on the notion of ransoming us from a god (or the devil in some texts) to whom we owe a debt.

This is what is called 'ontological debt', that is, the debt we owe to our parents, family, society, the planet, and 'God' for being brought into the world and raised to adulthood. Our debt to the planet is unending. Trying to quantify this type of debt by putting a monetary figure on it, or even to see money as in any way relevant to such a debt, is clearly not a rational thing to do. The appropriate response to this type of debt is respect for the people involved and conservation of the planet's natural resources. Many traditional cultures have interpreted this point of view to mean that one cannot own the land or its resources as they actually belong to the whole community.

Debt became more and more of a problem in the second and first millennia BCE, with vast numbers of people being reduced to debt peonage and finally slavery. Early empires would take periodic steps to cancel debt in order to resolve the mounting social crisis. This is the origin of the Jubilee Year described in Leviticus 25:8–13, which required that every 50 years, all debts would be cancelled and all Jewish slaves would be freed (though not foreign slaves). This is also why usury, the practice of charging interest on a debt, was outlawed in the Hebrew Scriptures (Deuteronomy 23:19–20) and considered a sin by the Christian Church up until the end of the Middle Ages. It is also why Jews were allowed to be bankers then, but not Christians. Jews could charge interest to Gentiles but not other Jews. Then, the local prince would periodically attack the Jews and rob them of most of their money. This was a very pragmatic solution to the religious prohibition.

Empires in particular thrive by inflicting debt on ordinary people. The breadth of Graeber's scholarship is such that he makes us aware that empires had developed in India and China as well as Rome. So the entire Eurasian continent, as well as North Africa, had found itself deeply oppressed by the economic burden of fuelling empires and their constant wars. It was such a serious human problem, that when all the empires collapsed, circa 500 CE, roughly within 200 years of one another, the religious movements in India, China, and the Middle East (both Christianity and Islam) found themselves necessarily focused on more just ways to manage economics in a society. This was a golden age of religions changing to ensure social justice for the common person. Communes, known as monasteries, brought the benefits of collectivizing labour for the good of all the participants, not the empire. Surplus produce was then meant to be given to the poor, though obviously as time went on, this aspect of their practice fell out of use.

This relief from the burden of debt on people, many of whom had found themselves reduced to slavery, was a vast improvement in the quality of life for the common man and woman. But the lure of power and control provided by large sums of money eventually overturned the more just society, and from 1450 onwards debt once again was promoted. The real favourite of bankers and pursuers of capital is compound interest. Graeber suggests that the inhuman destruction of the native population in Mexico by Cortés and others in the 1500s was due to the pressure he was under to produce a profit because he had taken out loans to finance his expedition. They were accruing compound interest by the day so he was in a frenzy to squeeze as much money out of the local economy as could be had.

The simplistic approach to economics that is fed to, and assumed by, ordinary people is totally misleading. It doesn't let us in on how rigged the game is and has always been. Bankers make money from thin air, that is, by advancing credit to people when they take out a loan. The bankers don't have that money in a box somewhere which they then hand over. It simply appears in the plus column of the ledger in the borrower's account. When the loan is paid back, with interest, the bankers receive money that they never actually had. In order for the lending system to work in favour of ordinary people, banks would need to be owned by the commonwealth which would benefit from lending money to local people. All profits made would then accrue to the commonwealth, not to private organisations running banks. But whenever countries begin to move in this direction, financial markets punish them severely lest they escape indebtedness to the owners of banks. Credit unions are the only real challenge to this system but they seem to be tolerated as long as they don't provide too much competition to the private banks.

Graeber noticed that the more people understand how money and debt actually work, the less willing they are to support a system that is stacked against the ordinary person. The apparent lack of alternatives, which neoliberalism tries to assert is the case, is not at all true. But people's ability to even imagine another way of doing business has been carefully curtailed by those who benefit handsomely from the current system.

Solutions?

Once we have a clearer understanding of what drives social injustice *and* what is required to promote emotional health in human beings, effective solutions become more obvious, though perhaps more fiercely resisted by those who currently own and run the world. Most obvious is that the capitalist system is inherently toxic, constantly promoting inequality and unsustainable use of natural resources. While educating people to the disadvantages of capitalism will help, they will not embrace such a change until their level of fear is eased and a halt put to manipulating it. Who will outlaw the telling of lies and the use of misleading spin in the media, and enforce it?

Any sustainable change towards justice in the world will require the healing of huge amounts of trauma held in the population. As long as a person is gripped by seemingly irresolvable fear, they will be unable to grow to the level of maturity required to sustain a more altruistic attitude in life. I think it is no accident, for example, that the most conservative part of the US, the South, was the section most impacted on by the violence of the American Civil War. The physical and economic trauma, not to mention the shame and humiliation they suffered, continues to fuel their rage. While this was unavoidable given their treatment of African Americans when they weren't willing to voluntarily give up slavery, the Civil War did not solve the problem in the long term. It merely made others feel like they had been made the victims.

Any long-term solution must find a way to not only change the rules and ensure people's physical and economic safety but also to heal the wounds of the past. This means educating people about the nature of trauma, how it is held in the body, and the means to release it. This needs to be combined with prioritizing the well-being of pregnant women so that their babies won't be born already traumatized. It has been amply demonstrated that if a pregnant woman suffers trauma, the neurotransmitters of that experience pass it on to her foetus. A genuine concern for family values demands the elimination of domestic violence and economic hardship for families and pregnant women.

Shortly after I started my first job as a psychotherapist, I did an I Ching reading for myself (using the *I Ching Workbook* by R. L. Wing), setting the following question: What is my life task? The first hexagram was entitled 'community' and the second was 'nourishing'. At the time my reaction to this was, 'What community am I meant to be nourishing?' It did not dawn on me at the time that I was working in a community mental health clinic. Indeed, for the vast majority of my professional life,

I have been working for employers that provided a service, often free, to members of the public. This is fairly unusual for psychotherapists who most often make their living in private practice. Yet my draw has been to work with people who could not otherwise afford my services.

This has provided me with a very satisfying life of work, though at the same time it has been very demanding. Particularly my last 13 years in the public service, where I was employed in a very under-resourced situation, I found myself working extremely hard. Yet this was also a very powerful way of living out my dedication to love and healing. Sitting with thousands of people, who had come to talk about the pain that had become unbearable for them, required of me a constant willingness to be open to that pain. In order to keep at it, I had to continually connect with a well of compassion within me. And those clients, who were exercising great courage in facing their own pain, powerfully inspired me to do the same for myself. It is in meeting our own pain that we get to know our self and thus to be our self.

From another angle, I have also become aware of the incredibly fortuitous coincidences in my life, which have generated a sense of being looked after by the universe. Initially, I had identified 1998 as the year I would move to Ireland. My plan was to start looking to make it happen that year. But in a conversation with a psychic she suggested that perhaps it would be better if I started a year earlier. It turned out that the process of moving over was much more complicated than I had anticipated. If I hadn't started a year earlier, it wouldn't have happened in 1998. Coincidently, my first employer in Ireland had started looking for someone to start a very specialized programme, for those who engage in self-harm, just at that time. I had been involved in such a programme in the Boston area, and so was well able to provide such a service. This was what secured me that first job. If I had started looking a year later, it would have already been filled.

When I had done as much for that employer as could be done in a healthy way, I needed to move on. Coincidently, for the very first time, a relatively new public health community service instituted a post for a psychotherapist in central Dublin, something that had not been done before. I successfully competed for that job. After a number of years, it became clear that it was time to move on. A short time later, someone contacted me to alert me to a totally new public primary care programme. It was advertising a post in Wicklow for my exact qualification, as a counselling psychologist rather than a clinical psychologist. It turns out to have been the only primary care job for a counselling psychologist in the country, all the rest having then been earmarked for clinical psychologists. Instead of an hour and a half commute, it entailed a 20-minute drive.

The same pattern played out with my housing situations. Initially, there was a severe accommodation shortage in Dublin. In addition, I was arriving in September, along with thousands of college students, all of us looking for a place to live. A friend noticed an ad for a room in a house close to where I would be working. Most of these would have been in a three-or four-bedroom house, rented by one student or young working person, who then advertised for more housemates. These situations were generally noisy, chaotic, party places. Instead, the place I came to was that of a single man who needed a little additional income to pay his mortgage. He was polite, friendly, and led a quiet life – no parties – perfect! After two years, he decided he wanted the house for his brother returning to Ireland to engage with the Celtic Tiger. Just at that point, a friend of a friend had heard that an older woman needed someone to stay in her house after her husband had died. Again, she turned out to be a very open-minded, freethinking person, and we got along famously. We still keep in touch.

Once I had a permanent and pensionable job, I was able to take on a mortgage. Again, a psychic said, forget about north of Dublin, that won't work for you; look to Wicklow and you'll find what you need. The first time I went into the local search engine for house buying, I entered what I could afford, and only one house came up. It was in Co. Wicklow. I moved on it immediately and was able to outbid the only competitor by just €500. It has worked out extremely well.

This kind of 'luck' is humbling and awe-inspiring. It has generated a very powerful sense of being in the right place at the right time. So even though I have taken some very large risks in my life, when it is clear to me that I am following that still, small voice within, I have learned to trust that it is the way to go.

Chapter 10

Relating to All That Is: Ecology

Now in the people that were meant to be green there is no more life of any kind. There is only shrivelled barrenness. The winds are burdened by the utterly awful stink of evil, selfish goings-on. Thunderstorms menace. The air belches out the filthy uncleanliness of the peoples. The earth should not be injured! The earth must not be destroyed!

Hildegard von Bingen (Twelfth century)

Whatever the original context of Hildegard's anguished cry it certainly captures our current plight in an amazingly prescient way. The earth is now headed for the destruction of the environment required to support human life; we are unlikely to survive. The earth itself will go on, and life will eventually reassert itself, though this may take millions of years as it did in previous die-offs. So much has been written about our current crisis from so many different angles that I will restrict my comments in this chapter to the spirituality which underlies it.

Functionally, humanity's domination of the earth would have begun with the Agrarian Revolution 12,000 years ago. As C.L. Flinders outlines in *Rebalancing the World* (2003) the shift from gathering/hunting to farming would have had immense implications for the attitudes and perceptions of the humans involved. She summarizes these in a table of two columns (p. 71), one headed The Values of Belonging, reflecting the reality of hunter-gatherers, and the other headed The Values of Enterprise, which was made possible by farming, with its immense food surpluses compared to gathering and hunting.

THE VALUES OF BELONGING	THE VALUES OF ENTERPRISE
Connection with land	Control and ownership of land
Empathic relationship with animals	Control and ownership of animals
Self-restraint	Extravagance and exploitation
Conservation	Change
Deliberateness	Recklessness and Speed
Balance	Momentum and High Risk
Expressiveness	Secretiveness
Generosity	Acquisitiveness
Egalitarianism	Hierarchy
Mutuality	Competitiveness
Affinity for alternative modes of knowing	Rationality
Playfulness	Businesslike sobriety
Inclusiveness	Exclusiveness
Nonviolent conflict resolution	Aggressiveness and violence
Spirituality	Materialism

The explosion of human population that abundant food made possible totally changed how people related to one another and to nature. The need to control nature, so that the harvest would be big enough to feed all the people who were born and survived because of the previous harvest, transforms the relationship into an adversarial one. Farmers would have seen their lives threatened by weather or pestilence, as indeed it was. From there, this attitude built into a need to exploit the mineral resources of the earth that are used to quantify the wealth accumulated by the farmers, or to make weapons to expand the amount of land controlled. The greater the wealth, the bigger the fear that it will be lost or that the power gained from it will be lost. From seemingly innocuous beginnings, all this has now spiralled out of control to the point where greed threatens our continued existence.

There were obvious advantages to the ability to generate a surplus and this has been celebrated, especially in entrepreneurial circles. But now, the natural limits inherent in living in the closed system of Planet Earth are beginning to constrict our room for survival, never mind expansion. This was inevitable even if there had continued to be some respect for nature and the physical environment. The lack of respect for nature has not only accelerated our nearing the limitations of that closed system but has also actively and intentionally promoted the poisoning of the environment, primarily for the pursuit of money. Think fracking.

To return to Robert Bellah's excellent work, *Religion in Human Evolution*, there is a particularly interesting and relevant section (pp. 146–159) describing the spirituality of some Australian Aboriginal people from the interior of that continent. Anthropologists have discovered during their time with these people something of how human consciousness functioned when it was deeply rooted to place in the land. Here are some excerpts that give a flavour of that way of being:

> [Their] understanding of being is oriented not so much to space (undifferentiated extension within which particular things occur) as to particular places, understood as conscious and alive—as living traces of ancestral beings. … [This mind frame] of rhythmic and abiding events occurring in particular places obviates the necessity of thinking about time and history. ... [T]he ancestral beings do not so much "create" the world … as form the world, for there is no idea of a beginning before creation, or even of creation. The forming activity of the ancestral beings is as much present as past. … Ubiety [thereness] so obliterates time

> that in the Dreaming, past, present, and future are not differentiated: there is only … "everywhen".

This means that all their stories that concern the balance of life and death, right action and wrong action, were held by the land that they had lived in for tens of thousands of years. Without that land their understanding of life would collapse. Bellah goes on to cite other researchers who observe that this manner of being in reality is only possible for as long as their place on the land is not threatened. When it is, their story falls apart and they suddenly 'fall into time and history … and the yearning for another time and another place begin'. When this displacement happened, with the arrival of Europeans and others, they began to use concepts like a 'Supreme Being' or a sky god, removed from any *place*.

> One feature of Aboriginal life has struck many of its most careful observers: the almost complete lack of imperial ambition. There are almost no cases of war for territorial expansion throughout the whole continent. This does not … mean that the Aboriginals weren't violent … for revenge, [etc.]. ... Ancestral Beings wandered all over the continent and their tracks could be traced through the territory of many groups. But the "owners" of sacred places were merely their custodians, and the places would not yield their fertility to those ignorant of the local ritual, so there was just no point in territorial expansion.

It is easy to see why this approach to spirituality would allow people to coexist and sustain themselves for the amount of time that humans had been around prior to the start of farming.

In terms of current eco-friendly spiritualities, it is still the approaches of native peoples that have the most to offer us. Even though they have also engaged in farming, they have not lost a sense of perspective. J. Diamond in *Guns, Germs, and Steel* (1999), helps to explain why it happened this way. He demonstrates that unless a population density is generated to a certain level, a more disembodied understanding of how reality works does not evolve. People who are in touch with the reality of the land can see quite clearly that if they don't actively work with nature to keep the land and water pure, their own existence is at risk. They honour their ontological debt to nature by respecting and working with the land. Because of this, it is Native Americans who have been at the forefront of opposing the construction of oil pipelines and fracking on their land.

Most of the Eurasian religions that came into being after the Agrarian Revolution have fallen into a dualism that sees material reality as either opposed to or less than spirit, or at the very least an illusion. This has meant that the material world has no inherent positive value within those spiritual systems. Yet without the material world we would not be able to live. Further, when matter is rejected by religious authorities, they give up any role in, or guidance of, its use. Those who know very clearly that control of natural resources gives them immense power are then free to do as they like with them. I would suggest that it has also led scientists, when they realized that religious leaders were incredibly ignorant about the material world, to champion it at the expense of realities that are different from the material world.

The absolutizing of the perceived world by science has directly contributed to the credibility of materialism. As previously outlined, however, quantum physics has demonstrated in a number of ways that the perceived world is a function of our psyches and the limitations of our biological organs of perception. The obvious disaster of a materialist approach to life is clear to anyone who doesn't hold that point of view, just as the pathology of Christianity is clear to atheists. But the adherents of both groups can't see that all points of view are arbitrary. There is no Holy Land of absolute truth. What each person needs is a story that supports them in a psychologically healthy way of life. We can't be healthy if we are destroying our environment any more than we can be healthy if we feel judged and threatened with eternal suffering.

Although Flinders opposes spirituality and materialism, I would continue to propose that materialism is a spirituality because it provides meaning to those whose life is shaped by the pursuit of wealth. Only if this is the case can materialism be seen to be the arbitrary position that it is. And as with any other spirituality it needs to be assessed on its ability to sustain psychologically healthy human beings. Then debates over which approach is true can be abandoned.

In the imagination of modern humans, 12,000 years seems like a long time, but in the larger picture, it is a very short period of time. Human beings have been around for at least half a million years. However, when decisions are made based on what's good for this quarter's profits, the larger picture doesn't enter the decision-making process in any shape or form. The progression into materialism is itself a product of humanity's need to control their reality, because since the Agrarian Revolution expansion has been seen as the only thing that matters. There has been no reflection on the impact or cost of a materialist approach to living: it must be the right way because it is the way we have gone, the way that is winning.

Even with an awareness of the pathology of the current economic system, it is very difficult for people to begin to shift their day-to-day lives to a more sustainable way of relating to nature. Most of us would be very hard-pressed to grow a significant portion of the food we need to survive for a year. Most non-agribusiness farmers specialize in only one or two areas of food production and most of those have to work outside the farm to bring in the cash necessary to purchase the goods and services required for modern living.

Even though time is very short in terms of the tipping point of climate change, there are options currently available which would begin to pull us back from the edge. But those who control the media are those who are profiting from the use of fossil fuels. Their commitment to business as usual blinds them to the plight of the planet. It remains to be seen whether the increase in the number of people waking up to the problem, due to its immediate impact on their lives, will be fast enough to override the message of the mainstream media. Fracking and extreme energy extraction have made a big contribution to the raising of awareness around the world. That, combined with the crisis of social injustice, may help rouse enough people to make a difference.

There are lots of movements currently underway, as can be found on the Popular Resistance website (popularresistance.org); becoming involved with them is one way to make a difference. There are those who feel that climate change is the most crucial focus, while others opt for social justice, economic reform, or political revolution. But it would be important to also consider the hidden assumptions in your way of life, or even simply the huge gaps in your awareness of nature. When I was young there were those lamenting the distancing from nature as more and more people were urbanized or suburbanized. Become aware of the phases of the moon as they are happening, celebrate the solstices and equinoxes as we circle the sun, or be aware of where your water comes from (wells, reservoirs, rivers). These are all ways that you can become more familiar with the details of your physical world and how you depend on it.

How do you relate to the land? Is it a subject or an object for you? Do you see it merely as an opportunity for making money or does it have something crucial to do with your community's history or even your survival on the planet?

Explore with an open mind some of the beliefs and customs of native peoples of your continent. Don't just assume that they were/are ignorant savages. They sustained their way of life for thousands of years longer than modern humans. How do you relate to insects, or rodents, or microbes? Many people have learned to fear these creatures. Overcoming such fears may require professional help, but at least getting to know more about them and their place and role in the world would be a step in the right direction. Places like Perelandra, a nature research centre in Virginia, or Findhorn in Scotland can help to provide a different picture of how we can relate to nature.

Perhaps one of the most important things you can do is to begin to resist the brainwashing that is advertising. This can't be done head on, so to speak, but requires the interruptive approach. It has been demonstrated that even those who pride themselves most on not being affected by advertising are, in fact, undermined by it. Therefore try things like putting the mute button on for all TV ads, getting an ad blocker on your web browser, or simply cultivating the closing or averting of your eyes whenever an ad is about to come into view. Advertising is a very effective technique for making you want things you don't need, yet also making you feel inadequate if you don't have them. Supporting any and all efforts to forbid the use of advertising would be another angle on this crucial battle for your mind.

As you can see from what I have shared, my life has been very interesting. It has also been very challenging at times, with a lot of moving around. This has involved much loss, along with new opportunities. My extended search to answer a question set in 1973, and then to come to grips with my sudden insight in Ghana in 1983, that I am God as Jesus was God, has led me to a more satisfactory version of both who Jesus was and what the divine is for me. I now hold that each of us is human – a unique, single individual – as well as divine, in that we participate in 'all that is' as an essential part of who we are. We are capable of working miracles of self-healing and revolutionizing our world with non-violence and compassion. We create our own reality through the belief system to which we subscribe and can change the one we were given by our initial circumstances in life. This requires a certain dying to our old (or earlier) self and moving into a more life-giving frame of reference based on love, compassion, and a regard for all that is.

I have learned over the decades how to resist the urge to make choices that prioritize short-term gain or self-soothing in favour of those that deepen a sense of dignity and self-compassion. Slow steps have taken me to a place in my self that allows me to be content with where I am, and to treasure those with whom I can comfortably share my being. I know that my practice of mindfulness is central to my ongoing development, as I continue to come to grips with undigested aspects of my self, as well as to find new meaning in my human being. I no longer struggle in the ways I did earlier in my life to make sense of life and death. It's OK to be me, and there is much to enjoy in each day.

I am at an age when death has begun to whittle away at my circle of friends. I believe we will meet again, but sometimes I also commune with them in quiet moments. I am really curious to see what will happen as I am crossing over from this reality into the one that brings smiles or looks of amazement to others at their time of letting go. The chaplain who sat with my father as he made that transition reported that he suddenly became alert. She asked him, 'Do you see someone?' He nodded, and she said, 'Go with them.' He died with a huge smile on his face.

I have more time now to explore history and understand the forces that have shaped us as people, for better and for worse. I am coming to believe that it is likely that the world as I have known it, with its billions of humankind, will most probably not be a feature of this planet for too many more centuries. Nevertheless, I still do as much as I can to fight for social justice and to reverse the ecological destruction that is gradually overwhelming a humanly liveable environment. Writing a book is a statement that life is still worth living and worth talking about with other people. Even if we cease to exist as a species on earth, I believe the universe will continue to evolve, as will we, however or wherever we will be.

This book has been many years in gestation. It has benefitted from that time, with the gradual accumulation of information and wisdom gained in my own living and the experience of others. The very act of putting words on my insights and self-reflection has contributed to my growth and self-articulation. If I had not written it, I would not have become me!

Chapter 11

Concluding Thoughts

> *Ask and it will be given to you; seek and you shall find; knock and the door will be opened to you.*
>
> *Matthew 7:7*

What do you take from all this?

The history of the term 'spirituality' is given by Carrette and King in their work *Selling Spirituality* (2004). The authors note that its use as we know it did not begin until the seventeenth century. It was around this time, in the aftermath of the Reformation, that people began to relate to God directly, having eliminated the priestly mediator. It is this awareness of ourselves as individuals which gives us the ability to choose and inhabit a spirituality rather than being a follower of a religion. Being a self-conscious individual is an important evolutionary step in being human. But it is also fraught with dangers and disadvantages. Once you have become self-conscious, however, there is no turning back. You can't decide that you'd rather be unconscious and pretend you don't know what's going on.

As highlighted previously, self-consciousness increases your level of fear because you are all the more aware of your vulnerability, your aloneness. Another difficulty with self-consciousness is that it is not complete. There is still a lot of you that you are totally unaware of: your unconscious. This part of you still exercises control over your behaviour, your thinking, and your emotions. Further, it makes it easy for others, who have some understanding of the unconscious, to manipulate you by pushing the buttons in your unconscious that produce an automatic, unconsidered response (see M. Dermot's 'How Big Data Becomes Psy Ops', 2017). This makes your self-consciousness rather precarious. It's like having only a torch in a very big, dark room and trying to make your way around without mishap.

An obvious solution to this state of affairs is to try, as much as possible, to discover what makes you tick. Looking into spirituality and where to go with it is a part of that journey of self-discovery. As you can see from earlier chapters, it is a journey that many people have been on and they have left us a record of where it has taken them. Prior to the emergence of the discipline of psychology, the record of people's journeying is found in their religions or their personal religious writings. In the past few centuries, the self-conscious study of the world and of human beings has provided an abundance of information on trying to make sense of our world and ourselves. The emergence of the natural sciences has given us a much better understanding of the world around us, to a point.

Psychology has focused specifically on how humans function. In its early stages, it tended to be solely physiologically based, with brain dissections and such, or else it tried to make sense of the unconscious and paranormal phenomena. Gradually, as the understanding of physiology improved with the use of modern research instruments, we have been able to see how our biology impacts on the ability of our consciousness to function in the here and now. That interface is a fascinating place. It has also shown that just because the body can't express consciousness as it usually does, does not mean that consciousness has gone or is compromised in its awareness.

Most recently, some biologists have finally started to take the quantum revolution into account. Bruce Lipton has been among the first to do so. His revised edition of his work *The Biology of Belief* (2015), has thus revolutionized our understanding of how our biology functions, debunking genetic determinism and clearly demonstrating that our cells are designed to respond to their environment. Quantum physics sees all reality as various expressions of energy. These expressions are a function of consciousness. This means that our cells respond to our consciousness, to our mind. Thus he comes to this powerful conclusion:

> My point is that you can choose what to see. You can filter your life with rose-colored beliefs that will help your body grow or you can use a dark filter that turns everything black and makes your body/mind more susceptible to disease. You can live a life of fear or live a life of love. You have the choice! But I can tell you that if you choose to see a world full of love, your body will respond by growing in health. If you choose to believe that you live in a dark world full of fear, your body's health will be compromised as you physiologically close yourself down in a protection response. (p. 137)

This means that what is usually dismissed as an 'all in your mind' placebo effect is actually an indicator of how our body functions at the quantum physics level. The full implications of a quantum-physics-informed biology are too numerous to convey here. I would enthusiastically recommend you add Lipton's work to your reading list.

Those who address people as conscious beings in psychotherapy have been aware for a long time that our biology isn't determined by traditional chemistry. Good doctors have known that things like motivation and positive attitude can play a major part in the healing process. Alternative healing techniques also take account of energies that run through the body carrying vital non-material components necessary for the rebalancing of the organism. Developmental research has demonstrated that there is a growth in individual consciousness throughout our life span – emotionally, morally, and spiritually – especially in terms of how we make meaning in our lives.

The notion that consciousness can be reduced to biology is a point of view held by those who maintain a materialist spirituality. The dangerous shortcomings of such a point of view are now becoming powerfully apparent. If we do not relate to the world at levels other than the material, the impact will be catastrophic, though it has taken millennia to finally see that this is the case.

I am assuming that you have read this book because you have questions about how to make meaning of your life and eventual death. Hopefully you have gained some insight into what is involved in crafting a psychologically healthy spirituality. You start wherever you are and begin to take stock of how you came to be there. What are the sources of your current beliefs, and what impact have they had on your life? Trying to answer such questions, as honestly as possible, is not easy. If you are lucky, perhaps there will be someone else you know who is interested in doing the same thing. It is very hard to find an already established group who has the same agenda, as most groups have already made choices about their meaning in life. Writing down your thoughts and questions on the topic can help your reflection process.

However, even if you are not dissatisfied with your current belief system, it is important to really look at what you believe, and identify how it influences how you live, and how it impacts others as well as the environment. The most unhelpful position is to think that you don't believe in anything. This blinds you to the fact that believing in 'nothing' is inherently impossible. The story you are telling yourself is that nothing is the meaning of your life, and you cannot see the functional storyline that underpins your life. Most often this is materialism and consumerism. It is whatever motivates you to get up out of bed each morning.

Most people, however, live in a system of one sort or another – a family, a workplace, social clubs – that make a large number of assumptions about the meaning of life. If you decide to strike out on your own, your journey can have difficult implications for your current social life. But coming to a meaning of your life is a really important task and is worth risking current contexts. However, it also takes years to fully articulate so it's important not to make precipitous choices. Slow and steady has a lot to recommend it, though a breaking point with your current context may eventually have to happen.

As you can see from past approaches to the meaning of life, keeping a balance between opposing poles is particularly important. There are many principles that are valid but only when balanced by the opposite point of view. The energies of the masculine and the feminine would be one basic example. Each is valid in its own right but if not balanced by the other, problems arise. Over the past 5,000 years or so, things have been unbalanced in favour of the masculine, and the impact of that is quite visible if you are trying to uphold the importance of the feminine. Another example would be the individual and the collective/community. Being an individual is very important if we are to make our contribution to the bigger picture. Yet if one pursues the rugged individualism often championed by capitalist societies, the lack of consideration for the group becomes inherently self-destructive in the long run.

Perhaps the most often repeated mistake in spiritualities has been the approach of dualism: exalting spirit and condemning matter. Again, this is a problem of balance, but one that has corrupted many otherwise apparently attractive spiritualities. It can be very subtly embedded so it is important to pay specific attention to this point. Any approach that engages in harsh asceticism, mortification of the flesh, or otherwise sees the body as less than consciousness or the soul/spirit is unhealthy psychologically. It also leads to a misogynist or sexist attitude to women, who are seen as either temptresses of the flesh, playthings or servants for men, or breeders for their dynastic ambitions. How one relates to the planet, to matter in its entirety, is also impacted by any kind of dualistic assumption.

Once I met a fellow who told me about a Buddhist sect which held that their more 'enlightened' members did not need to treat the less so with respect or fairness. This social arrangement would attract many of that oft met duo: aggressor and victim. Few groups are so obvious in their lack of moral maturity, but if you hold social justice as an important value, you will be spared a sojourn in such a group.

And even the very yardstick of psychology which I am using to assess a healthy spirituality has its own problems. There is no one psychological understanding of what it means to be human, and psychology can be used to torture as well as to heal. It is massively used in advertising to make you buy what you don't need, to make you believe buying is the meaning of life. It takes much discernment and experimenting with points of view to ascertain whether they are leading you to health or to increased fear.

Developing a mindfulness practice is a relatively simple and stabilizing thing to do. It will help you to discover your self moment by moment. It must be done with non-judging of your self, simply accepting what you find in the moment. Even when you are judging your self, you become aware of that, and simply accept that that is what is happening, just now. Then you can renew your choice to stop doing that.

If you find yourself becoming deeply upset and panicked when you try to do your mindfulness practice, it could be an indication that you are suffering from untreated trauma. You will need to find a good psychotherapist who works with the body to release trauma. Anyone who simply tries to 'talk you through it' is to be avoided.

This journey is a very arduous one, and you will need support on it. You will need to find others who are on a similar journey. Non-religiously based mindfulness groups can be helpful for this. But a Christian or a Buddhist group will lead you down a road which has specific definitions of your experience. If you can stay conscious of that, you may be able to make use of the group if no other is available.

Reading is also a helpful option for exploring the way others have made meaning of life. In previous chapters I have mentioned many books I found useful in my own explorations. There are many more for you to discover, and many more yet to be published that will be useful.

If you have, or intend to have, children, educate yourself about the developmental emotional needs of children. T. Lewis et al.'s *A General Theory of Love* (2001) or S. Gerhardt's *Why Love Matters* (2014) are good resources for this. It is very difficult not to pass on the wounds of your family of origin but trying not to do so can make a difference. Remember that you do the best you can, and after that it will be up to each child to take up their own healing journey. Each of us comes into this life with our own agenda and parents are the facilitators not the determiners of their children's lives.

Most of all trust that life will lead you where you need to go. Even when at times it looks like a disaster, something useful is likely to come of it. By the time I was 40 I had adopted the motto that 'whatever happens, happens for the best'. I don't always like to be reminded of that when I'm in the middle of some disaster or other, but I have found it to be true for me.

Lastly, remember that life is an adventure, so be sure to have some fun. Now off you go on your yellow brick road ...

Further Reading

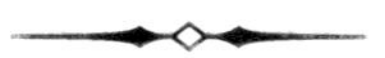

Abbott, E., 2015. *Flatland.* Norfolk, Chiron Academic Press.

Aeschylus, 1975. *The Oresteia.* Translated from Greek by R. Fagles. New York: Bantam.

Altemeyer, R., 2006. *The Authoritarians.* Self-published. [online] Available at: http://members.shaw.ca/jeanaltemeyer/drbob/TheAuthoritarians.pdf [Accessed 13 February 2017].

Alter, A., 2017. *Irresistible: Why We Can't Stop Checking, Scrolling, Clicking and Watching.* London: Penguin Random House.

Baigent, M. and Leigh, R., 1997. *The Elixir and the Stone.* New York: Dell.

Barger, R. N., 2000. A Summary of Lawrence Kohlberg's Stages of Moral Development. [online] Available at: https://www.csudh.edu/dearhabermas/kohlberg01bk.htm [Accessed 13 February 2017].

Bellah, R., 2011. *Religion in Human Evolution.* Cambridge, MA: Belknap Press (an imprint of Harvard University Press).

Bolte Taylor, J., 2008. *My Stroke of Insight.* New York: Penguin Books.

Bradshaw, J., 1991. *Homecoming.* New York: Bantam Dell Publishing Group.

Bruce, A., 2005. *Beyond the Bleep.* New York: Disinformation Books.

Carrette, J. and King, R., 2004. *Selling Spirituality.* New York: Routledge.

Libreria Editrice Vaticana, 1992. *Catechism of the Catholic Church.* Rome: Citta del Vaticano.

The Century of the Self, 2002. BBC documentary film series by A. Curtis. UK.

Chopra, D., 2003. *SynchroDestiny.* London: Rider.

Cockell, J., 1993. *Yesterday's Children.* London: Piatkus Books.

Cohen, P., 2016. Wealth Inequality Rising Fast, Oxfam Says, Faulting Tax Havens. *New York Times,* 18 January 2016. [online] Available at https://www.nytimes.com/2016/01/19/business/economy/wealth-inequality-rising-fast-oxfam-says-faulting-tax-havens.html [Accessed 17 March 2017].

Critchley, S., 2012. *Faith of the Faithless: Experiments in Political Theology*. New York: Verso.

Dermot, M., 2017. How Big Data Becomes Psy Ops and Tilts World Towards Its Own Aims. [online] Available at: https://educationalchemy.com/> or <https://popularresistance.org/how-big-data-becomes-psy-ops-and-tilts-world-towards-its-own-aims/ [Accessed 13 February, 2017].

Diamond, J., 1999. *Guns, Germs, and Steel*. New York: W.W. Norton and Company.

Donoghue, F., 2008. *The Last Professors*. New York: Fordham University Press.

Douglas-Klotz, N., 2001. *The Hidden Gospel*. Wheaton, IL: Quest Books.

Flinders, C. L., 2003. *Rebalancing the World*. San Francisco: Harper.

Fowler, J. W., 1995/1981. *Stages of Faith: The Psychology of Human Development and the Quest for Meaning*. New York: HarperCollins, College Division.

Gerhardt, S., 2014. *Why Love Matters: How Affection Shapes a Baby's Brain.* 2nd ed. New York: Routledge.

Gieser, S., 2005. *The Innermost Kernel*. New York: Springer Verlag.

Gilligan, C., 1982. *In a Different Voice*. Harvard, MA: Harvard University Press.

Graeber, D., 2011. *Debt: The First 5,000 Years*. New York: Melville House.

Grünwald, I., 1980. *Apocalyptic and Merkavah Mysticism*. Leiden: Brill.

Gudrais, E., 2011. What we know about wealth. *Harvard Magazine*, Nov–Dec, 2011. [online] Available at: http://harvardmagazine.com/2011/11/what-we-know-about-wealth [Accessed 13 February 2017].

Hanegraaff, W. J., 1997. *New Age Religion and Western Culture: Esotericism in the Mirror of Secular Thought*. New York: SUNY Press.

Hanh, T. N., 2001. *Anger: Buddhist Wisdom for Cooling the Flames*. London: Rider.

Hartmann, T., 2004. *The Last Hours of Ancient Sunlight*. New York: Three Rivers Press.

Haughton, R., 1981. *The Passionate God*. New York: Paulist Press.

Herman, E. S. and Chomsky, N., 2011. *Manufacturing Consent: The Political Economy of the Mass Media*. New York: Pantheon. [online cartoon summary] Available at: https://www.youtube.com/watch?v=34LGPIXvU5M [Accessed 6 March 2017].

Kohlberg, L., 1984. *The Psychology of Moral Development*. San Francisco: Harper and Row.

Kolk, van der, B., 2014. *The Body Keeps the Score*. New York: Penguin Books.

Krishna, G., 1974. *Kundalini: The Evolutionary Energy in Man*. Boston: Shambhala.

Leininger, B. & A., 2010. *Soul Survivor*. New York: Grand Central Publishing.

Levine, P., 2008. *Healing Trauma*. Boulder, CO: Sounds True Inc.

Levine, P., 2010. *In an Unspoken Voice*. Berkeley, CA: North Atlantic Books.

Levine, P. and Phillips, M., 2012. *Freedom from Pain*. Boulder, CO: Sounds True Inc.

Lewis, T., Amini, F. and Lannon, R., 2001. *A General Theory of Love*. New York: Vintage Books.

Lipton, B., 2015. *The Biology of Belief*. New York: Hay House Inc.

Lucas, S., 2005. *Past Life Dreamwork*. Rochester, VT: Bear and Company.

Malone, M. T., 2000. *Women and Christianity*, vol. 1. Dublin: Columba Press.

McMahon, P. F., 1987 to 1996. *The Grand Design*, 5 vols. Dublin: Auricle Enterprises.

Mindell, A., 2000. *The Quantum Mind*. Portland, OR: Lao Tse Press.

Mindell, A., 2000. *Dreaming While Awake*. Charlotteville, VA: Hampton Roads Publishing Company.

Moncrieff, S., 2006. *God: A User's Guide*. Dublin: Poolbeg Press.

Myers, I. B., McCaulley, M., H., Quenk, N. L. and Hammer, A. L., 1998. *MBTI Manual: A Guide to the Development and Use of the Myers-Briggs*

Type Indicator. 3rd ed. Washington, DC: Consulting Psychologists Press.

Newton, M., 1994. *Journey of Souls*. St Paul, MN: Llewellyn Publishing.

Newton, M., 2000. *Destiny of Souls*. St Paul, MN: Llewellyn Publishing.

Newton, M., 2004. *Life between Lives*. St Paul, MN: Llewellyn Publishing.

Ogden, P., 2006. *Trauma and the Body*. New York: WW Norton & Company.

Patai, R., 1990. *The Hebrew Goddess*. Detroit, MI: Wayne State University Press.

Porete, M., 1993. *The Mirror of Simple Souls*. (Classics of Western Spirituality) Translated from Old French by E. Babinsky. New York: Paulist Press.

Post, van der, L., 1977. *Lost World of the Kalahari*. New York: Harcourt, Brace and Company.

Reid, N., 2015. Ancient Aboriginal stories preserve history of a rise in sea level, in C. Moseley, ed. *OGMIOS Newsletter* 58 Dec. 2015, ISSN 1471CO382. [online] Available at: http://www.ogmios.org/ogmios/Ogmios_058.pdf [accessed 13 February, 2017].

Schucman, H., 1976. *A Course in Miracles*. New York: Foundations for Inner Peace.

Siedentop, L., 2014. *Inventing the Individual*. London: Penguin.

Schillebeeckx, E., 1980. *Ministry*. London: SCM Press Ltd.

Schüssler, E., 2015. *Miriam's Child, Sophia's Prophet*, 2nd ed. New York: T & T Clarke.

Vaughan-Lee, L. ed., 2013. *Spiritual Ecology*. Point Reyes, CA: The Golden Sufi Center.

Versluis, A., 1998. *The Philosophy of Magic*. Boston, MA: Arkana Paperbacks.

What the Bleep Do We Know? 2004. [Film] Directed by W. Arntz, B. Chasse, and M. Vicente. USA: Captured Light and Lord of the Wind Films, LLC.

Wilbur, K., 2001. *The Eye of Spiri*t. Boston: Shambhala.

Williamson, M., 1992. *A Return to Love*. New York: Harper/Collins

Wing, R. L., 1979. *The I Ching Workbook*. New York: Doubleday.

Wolf, F. A., 2001. *Mind into Matter: A New Alchemy of Science and Spirit*.

Needham, MA: Moment Point Press Inc.

Wright, M. S., 1987. *Behaving as if the God in All Life Mattered*. Jeffersonton, VA: Perelandra.

Wright, M. S., 1993. *Garden Workbook I*. 2nd ed. Jeffersonton, VA: Perelandra.

Wright, M. S., 1990. *Garden Workbook II*. Jeffersonton, VA: Perelandra.

Wright, M. S., 1995. *Dancing in the Shadows of the Moon*. Jeffersonton, VA: Perelandra.

Young, J., 2004. *The Cost of Certainty*. London: Darton, Longman & Todd.

Young, J., 2007. *The Violence of God and the War on Terror*. London: Darton, Longman & Todd.

Index

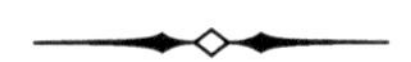

CPSIA information can be obtained
at www.ICGtesting.com
Printed in the USA
LVOW07s1603310817
547116LV00006B/953/P

9 781911 013884